"To drop a plumb line into the depths of life, to find thereby the great emotions common to all mankind and to express them so that all mankind will understand the expression — this, I think is what art is for."

Gutzon Borglum

Lincoln's father had taught him that every statue should tell a story, that it should portray a moment in our nation's history, or in the life of a man, that is worth remembering. In 1961, twenty years after Gutzon Borglum's death, his son, Lincoln, created this portrait bust to tell an unforgettable story of the devotion between a father and a son.

James de la Mothe Borglum

Gutzon Borglum

The Man Who Carved a Mountain

Willadene Price

Illustrated
With 60
Photographs

Dedicated To
Lincoln and Mary Ellis

ISBN: 0-914440-04-7
Library of Congress Catalog Card Number: 61-13983
Copyright© 1961 by Willadene Price
All Rights Reserved
1983 Edition

Cover design by Robert Altemus
Printed in the United States of America

Contents

The Author

Willadene Price, like most visitors, was awestruck when she first gazed on the four Presidential faces carved on Mt. Rushmore. It was more than 20 years, however, before she undertook to write this biography of the creator of the giant sculpture, Gutzon Borglum. While she was researching her first book, *Bartholdi and the Statue of Liberty*, she learned that it was Borglum who had re-designed Miss Liberty's torch so that it would give off a glitter that could really be seen. The more she learned about the erratic, controversial, lovable genius, the more eager she became to write about him. Telling his story and reliving through his artistry many of America's finest hours gave her profound joy.

A native of Nebraska, Mrs. Price lives with her husband in Alexandria, Va., where she is now completing a biography of Daniel Chester French.

The Illustrations

I wish to express profound gratitude to Lincoln Borglum for allowing me access to Gutzon Borglum's magnificent collection of photographs as well as to his own personal collection of pictures. All the pictures not otherwise credited, forty-nine of the fifty-eight which appear in the book, came from the Borglum Collections. While many of these photographs were taken by Lincoln Borglum, credit is due the following photographers: Beeville Studio, Beeville, Texas, for the frontispiece and the illustration at the bottom of page 215; Susan French, Santa Monica, California, for the picture on page 36; Brown Brothers for the one on page 77; Charles d'Emery, Publisher's Photo Service, Inc., Stamford, Connecticut, for pictures which appear on pages 120, 123, 124, 145, 147, and 163; Bell Photo, Rapid City, for the pictures on pages 160 and 182; Verne's Photo Shop for the picture on page 209.

For the pictures not in the Borglum Collection, I wish to express sincere thanks to The Joslyn Art Museum for the illustration on page 27; to Mrs. Mary Ellis Vhay for pictures on pages 48 and 98; to the Library of Congress for the photograph on page 82, which was taken by Waldon Fawcett, Washington, D. C.; to America's Independent Electric Light and Power Companies for the picture on page 91, which was supplied by N. W. Ayer and Son, Inc.; to Guy E. March, South Dakota School of Mines, for the picture on page 158; to the National Park Service for the picture on page 172, which was taken by Photo Art Center, Rapid City; to the Mount Rushmore National Memorial Society for the picture at the bottom of page 190, by Bell Photo; to Charles d'Emery, Manugian Studios, South Norwalk, Connecticut, for the photograph which appears on page 193.

Willadene Price

Illustrations

Gutzon Decides to be an Artist

1

James Borglum, a fine Latin and Greek scholar and a third-year medical student, was the first of the ancient Borglums to leave Denmark for America. In 1864, when he was twenty-five, his father, Gutzon Borglum, died. Angered by a family disagreement over the division of property, James and his young wife left Denmark. In America, they lingered but a day or so in New York City and then headed for the West. But they got only as far as Bear Lake on the border between Utah and Idaho. Here a number of small settlements were already established and the young pioneers, weary of long months of hardships, decided to go no further. In exactly which settlement they chose to build their log hut is not known. But it was in this log hut that John Gutzon de la Mothe Borglum was born on March 25, 1867.

When Gutzon, as he was always called, was sixty years old, he met a cousin who told him he had been born in 1871. Gutzon promptly changed his birthdate saying, "I am going to accept these years as a straight gift and live by them." However, church and family records indicate that he was born in 1867.

Shortly after Gutzon's birth the family decided to move

9

south into Utah. They established themselves in Ogden and three days before Christmas, in 1868, Solon was born.

Gutzon's only recollection of his very early childhood was a hazy memory of a day when his mother called him and Solon in from play, kissed them, and said goodbye to them. Then she walked out the door and never came back. By the time Gutzon was old enough to want an explanation, there was already Ida, a stepmother, and somehow he couldn't bring himself to ask his father any questions. His father insisted that he call his stepmother "Mama," but he was a grown man before he did so willingly.

By 1874 James Borglum had five sons and a baby daughter. With his three years of medical training in Denmark as a background, he had eked out a meager living taking care of the sick. But he wanted something more for his family. To be a success as a doctor he knew he would have to obtain a degree in medicine. He moved his family to St. Louis, Missouri, and somehow managed the year of work and study necessary to get his degree from the St. Louis Homeopathic Medical College.

He heard there was need for a doctor in Fremont, Nebraska, described to him as a "fast growing" town. It was located at the junction of the valleys of the Platte and Elkhorn Rivers and on the mainline of two railways—the *Fremont, Elkhorn & Missouri Valley* and the *Union Pacific.* The thirty-five-year-old doctor decided that Fremont was a good place to begin his professional career.

Doctor Borglum was not disappointed in Fremont. This was no ordinary frontier town. It boasted two daily newspapers and a weekly. Its dusty Main Street was lined with thriving business houses. Cole and Pilsbury's Wholesale and Retail Store handled the finest quality cutlery, stoves, tinware, paints, glass, and sundry merchandise. There was a photographer's studio that would have been a credit to an eastern city, a large milling company, and a brick manufacturing company.

It was summer when the family arrived in Fremont. School was closed, but the Borglum boys quickly made friends. They swam with the others at Rawhide Creek. It was called Rawhide, they were told, because on its banks a buffalo hunter who had shot an Indian girl was tied to a cottonwood tree and skinned alive by revengeful squaws.

They also played a game of American and British soldiers, fighting furious mock battles with tall, strong weeds as spears.

Most of the boys in Fremont had ponies of their own, many of them bought from the Pawnee Indians who brought in prairie ponies to sell at auction. The first time Gutzon went to the auction he saw a little steel-gray mare that he wanted. Before Gutzon could reach the mare, the Indian owner had roped and thrown her and was sitting on her head calling for bids. "I'll take her, I'll take her," shouted Gutzon. "How much?" asked the Indian. Gutzon had his entire savings with him. "Fifty cents," said Gutzon.

The Indian started to call for another bid. Then he took another look at Gutzon and got up instead. "You got a good bargain, boy," he said, as he handed Gutzon the rope. "This pony is worth sixty-five cents."

It didn't matter to Gutzon whether he got a bargain or not. He would have paid more for the pony if he had had any more. He tugged gently at the rope and after a few moments the mare hesitantly followed him. When he got home he turned the pony loose in the corral. She flung her head back and away she went. With her mane and tail flying Gutzon thought she looked as if she had wings.

For days Gutzon pushed feed and water under the fence for his pony, always talking gently to her. One day he went into the corral and she didn't run away from him, even when he stroked her. A week or so later, she willingly let him put a rope around her neck and lead her around. Then one day when he was sitting on the fence admiring her, she sidled up to him and he slipped over on her back. In later years, Gutzon always said he never "broke" a horse but he "gentled" them into letting him ride. His little steel-gray mare was only the first of many horses that Gutzon Borglum "gentled."

The days were not all happy ones for Gutzon. It seemed to him that whenever he was in sight of the house his stepmother was after him to do some chore. She made him bring in all the wood for the cook stove and sometimes he thought his back would break from all the buckets of water he had to pump and carry to the house.

One hot day when the boys were all starting off to swim, Gutzon's stepmother called him back to go on an errand. Gutzon was hurt and upset but he started to do the errand. Then an idea came to him. He wondered why he hadn't thought of it long before. He would run away!

In two days Gutzon didn't get very far from home. He spent most of his time resting and wishing for something to eat. A sheriff caught up with him and brought him back, and that homecoming was something to remember. Doctor Borglum was away on a call at the time so Gutzon's stepmother let an Uncle, who was visiting, tie Gutzon to a post in the stable yard and whip him. Gutzon wouldn't have minded the whipping so much if his three stepbrothers, Miller, August, and Arnold, hadn't been allowed to watch. Solon, his own brother, ran and hid in the barn.

Gutzon was really glad when it was time for school to

*Ida, Gutzon Borglum's
stepmother*

open, so that he could get away from scoldings at home for part of the day.

At the Fremont Public School, lower grade pupils met together in one room. Gutzon thought it much more fun to watch the fifth-graders draw maps on the blackboard than to pay attention to the dull repetition of words in his third reader. Finally the teacher decided to punish Gutzon by making him draw a map of Nebraska on the blackboard. Gutzon was frightened and embarrassed when the teacher handed him the chalk. But as soon as he started to draw, he forgot everything else.

When he stood aside to let his classmates see the finished map, there were loud gasps of admiration from everyone, including the teacher. Gutzon had surprised even himself! He had no idea drawing was such fun.

Although the teacher was pleased with Gutzon's maps and frequently shamed the older pupils by comparing their work unfavorably with his, it didn't occur to her, or to anyone else, that Gutzon might have a special talent.

For awhile Gutzon was quite content to draw maps. Then he began to try his hand at other things. By the end of the school year the margins of all his textbooks were cluttered with sketches, especially of horses.

His stepmother had now found a new cause for scoldings. She said that Gutzon spent all his time scribbling pictures instead of helping out around the house. She often remarked, "Gutzon will never amount to anything."

Gutzon fixed himself a place in a corner of the cellar where, once in awhile, when he felt like being all by himself, he could hide. He had a few water colors and he kept them down there too. One time he painted a picture on the lid of an old cigar box. He gave it to Anna, his stepsister. At the time, no one seemed to have admired it, but many years later Anna wrote to Gutzon, "I am still using the cigar box you painted for me for a sewing box."

Doctor Borglum was not as severe with Gutzon. Perhaps he remembered how, as a boy, he much preferred to make wood carvings than to study Latin and Greek. As Gutzon grew older, Doctor Borglum took him with him more and more often during the summer around the countryside. Gutzon enjoyed the long buggy rides over the rutty, tree-lined country roads. He liked to stop along the way to visit or to have a bite to eat with a friendly farm family. Gutzon became a real help to his father. By the time he was ten or eleven, he could make a tourniquet out of a rope or an old rag, if necessary. He could hold open a wound while his father picked out gunshot. And he was quite skillful at handing his father medicine or instruments in an emergency.

At school, though Gutzon never won in a spelling bee, he could name all the presidents of the United States and he never missed a line when asked to recite the Preamble to the Constitution. He was fascinated by the exciting stories of the growth and expansion of America. For the most part his school marks were poor; nevertheless, his father evidently felt that he showed some academic promise, because when Gutzon was ready to enter high school, Doctor Borglum sent him to a boarding school in St. Marys, Kansas.

The teachers at the St. Mary's School quickly recognized Gutzon's artistic talent. They put him to work drawing saints and angels. Gutzon would have preferred to draw horses but was pleased to receive any encouragement. At first he thought his teachers and fellow students were making fun of him when they suggested he choose art as a career. Gradually he gained confidence. These were his friends. They honestly did not think he was lazy because he liked to draw pictures.

Gutzon finished St. Mary's School determined to begin his life at home as an artist. By now, home was no longer in Fremont. A year after Gutzon started school in Kansas, his father had had an opportunity to take over a practice in Omaha, Nebraska. By this time, there were eight children and Doctor Borglum thought it would be easier to support them in a wealthier community.

On the trip home from Kansas Gutzon decided to stop over in Kansas City to visit a leading art store. He thought he might buy a few supplies to be ready to start his art career. He got so excited at the wonderful array of artist's supplies and bought so many tubes of paint that he didn't have enough money left for his train fare home. Not in the least distressed, Gutzon simply got on the train, told the conductor what had happened, and was permitted to ride free.

Gutzon had not reckoned with Doctor Borglum and his stepmother. They had no time to waste on the foolish whims of a boy who wanted to be an artist. They had given him a better than average education and they felt it was time now for him to go to work and help out with expenses at home.

Said his stepmother, "Whoever heard of an artist—even a real one—much less a sixteen-year-old boy, making a living."

Gutzon had no alternative. He had no money and no place else to go. So he went to work in a machine shop. He had heard that opportunities for artists were greater in the Far West. He determined to leave as soon as he could save enough money to make the trip to California. Meantime, Albert Rothery, an artist in Omaha, took an interest in Gutzon. He admired Gutzon's sketches of wild, spirited horses. Gutzon even went occasionally to his studio for a lesson.

When Gutzon accumulated a little money he told his father of his plan to go west. Doctor Borglum himself was disheartened over the way things were going in Omaha. Fabulous stories of opportunities in the Golden West excited him as much as they did Gutzon. In any event, whether it was for Gutzon's sake, or for his own, he found it easy to pull up stakes. He sold his home in Omaha in the spring of 1884 and the entire Borglum family boarded the train for Los Angeles.

Gutzon was seventeen years old. He had firmly made up his mind that no matter how hard he had to work or what he might have to give up, nothing would ever keep him from pursuing a career in art.

An early sketch of horses by Borglum

To Fame on Horseback

2

WITH MIDWESTERNERS pouring into the city by the hundreds, Los Angeles was in the midst of a gigantic real estate boom. Real estate offices lined the two most important streets, Spring and Main, and carried on their business like so many side shows. Some had bands playing to attract customers. Others offered free lunches.

Doctor Borglum quickly bought a newly built frame house on Temple Street. Like all the others, the Borglum house was covered from eaves to porch rail with wooden scrolls and curlycues.

Gutzon soon met a group of other aspiring artists. Los Angeles seemed to be a mecca for artists and writers, young and old. There were dozens of little hole-in-the-wall art shops where paintings in fancy gingerbread frames sold for five dollars each and even less. Any painter who could possibly scrape together enough money rented himself a big, bare room, called it a studio, and plastered the walls with his efforts. Gutzon could hardly wait until he had enough money to do the same.

Jobs were not plentiful. Gutzon finally got himself apprenticed to a lithographer at practically no pay. However, he

17

thought the job offered opportunity for quick advancement. After six months he got so adept at engraving and designing upon stone that he felt he was good enough to have a substantial increase in pay. The owner of the firm thought otherwise, so Gutzon, who felt he was wasting his talents on a most unappreciative boss, quit.

Gutzon was discouraged. He had no money. He was no closer to a career in art than he had been in Omaha. He got no sympathy at home either. Doctor Borglum, who was having a struggle to support his large family, was amazed when Gutzon told him he had quit his job. "I cannot understand, Gutzon," he said, "why you would quit a job, even a small paying one, when you had nothing else in sight."

How could Gutzon explain that he simply could not do good work when he felt he was unjustly treated? Gutzon didn't much like working for someone else anyway. He decided to try to find a job where he could be freer to use his own ideas.

A friend had taken a job as a fresco painter and he suggested that Gutzon work with him until he could find something better. Fresco painting consisted of painting walls and then panelling them with a six- or eight-inch border of fancy painted scrolls and angel heads in the corners. Gutzon got so good at fresco painting that builders of new houses began to ask for him by name. In fact, he was doing so well that he began to look around for a room of his own where he could establish a studio. He was anxious to put some of the magnificent California scenery on canvas. He was fascinated by the tales of early California and he wanted to record some of that history on canvas too.

To Doctor Borglum and his wife, Ida, Los Angeles held no such fascination. After two years, they still saw only a glittering, raucous city with a shifting population of get-rich-quick speculators. "This is no place to raise a family," said Doctor Borglum. Ida shared his belief and they decided to move back to Nebraska. By now another boy had joined the family. There were now nine children, three girls and six boys. Seven of the children made the trip with their parents back to Nebraska. Gutzon, at least for the moment, felt he wanted to live forever in California. His stepbrother, August, who had a job with a newspaper, wanted to be a musician and he felt he would have more chance for success in Los Angeles than in Omaha.

August rented a room near his work and Gutzon was taken in by a friendly neighbor. Gutzon paid for his board and room by painting portraits of all the members of the family. Fortunately there were six children, and since Gutzon could paint only in his free time, it took him many months to do all the pictures. In a short while August tired of life in a rooming house and joined the family in Omaha.

Gutzon had no thought of returning to Omaha. He was much too busy searching for a room that would be suitable for a studio. There were plenty of rooms available but they were either too small or the rent was too high. Finally, Gutzon did find a place that suited him. It was a big, barny room in a ramshackle building high on a hill on Fort Street. Gutzon thought it was a beautiful spot. From his window he could see blocks of green pepper trees, their delicate green foliage bedecked like so many Christmas trees with red and green berries.

Now that he had his own studio, Gutzon, at nineteen, felt he was really on his way toward a life of fame as an artist. He spent all the money he had saved on needed art supplies. Then, as if to make up for years he felt he had lost, he spent every free moment painting. Sometimes he worked far into the night. Before long the walls of his studio were covered with sketches and paintings of California sunsets, magnificent trees, the sea, moonlit nights, Indians, cowboys, and horses of every description.

Visitors began to drop in. Gutzon was especially pleased to welcome Charles F. Lummis, who was then a reporter for the Los Angeles *Times*. Lummis was one of the most colorful characters of the West. He had walked from Ohio to California in 1884, stopping here and there to absorb the history of the country and to send weekly stories of his adventures to the *Times*. He was tremendously interested in Gutzon's efforts to preserve on canvas the beauty and the history of California. He strode around the studio, gesturing his approval with his big white sombrero. Later, in a magazine called *Land of Sunshine*, that he edited, he wrote that Gutzon's "paintings had many shortcomings and showed lack of art education; yet there was in them a creative breadth which promised to make him heard from."

None of Gutzon's visitors bought any paintings, but they all admired his enthusiasm, and they invariably sent their friends to see his work. The mere fact that visitors came to look was all the encouragement Gutzon needed. He gave up his fresco painting job, and hung a sign outside his studio door that read, "J. G. Borglum, Artist and Instructor." In an amazingly short time Gutzon had enough pupils to pay the rent. Mostly they were older men and women who "always thought they wanted to learn to paint, but just hadn't had an opportunity before."

Gutzon had never worried about his lack of formal art training, but when he tried to teach others, he began to realize his own limitations. Enthusiasm, he found, was no substitute for training. He was aware, too, that many wealthy Californians were paying high prices for portraits, and he was anxious to win enough recognition to get some of those commissions. He decided he would go to the San Francisco Art Association to study. As usual, he had no money, but a few of his pupils paid several months' fees in advance to enable him to go.

By the time Gutzon had traveled the nearly five hundred miles of scenic wonderland between Los Angeles and San Francisco, he had mentally sketched a dozen paintings. As the panting little locomotive had puffed its way along a narrow ledge of mountainside, Gutzon's vivid imagination went back to the days of '49. "What a picture it must have been," said Gutzon to a fellow traveler, "to see a stage coach go thundering along these precipices."

Gutzon's enthusiasm was even greater when he reached San Francisco—a metropolis of three hundred thousand people. "What a magnificent city!" he exclaimed to the driver as he boarded one of the little cable cars that honeycombed the hills on which the city was built.

Gutzon went straight to the San Francisco Art Association on Pine Street and enrolled in a class taught by the veteran painter Virgil Williams. At the Association, he met a young Norwegian artist named Martin Borgord and the two struck up an immediate friendship. Martin called Gutzon "Borgie." It was the first time Gutzon had ever had a nickname and he liked it.

It was Martin who first introduced Gutzon to William Keith, the "Grand Old Man of California Painting." All artists in San Francisco, at one time or another, visited the studio of the white-haired, white-bearded Keith. Gutzon went back again and again. He didn't mind that sometimes Keith was moody and gruff. "You must paint with your emotions," Keith told Gutzon. "When you are in a rage," he said, "is the time to paint a frothing sea, not fleecy white clouds in a calm blue sky." Keith reveled in nature and Gutzon thought his picture of California oaks against a darkening sky one of the most magnificent paintings he had ever seen.

Both Keith and Williams advised Gutzon to do more painting outdoors. So Gutzon spent days at Meigg's Wharf trying to capture the spirit of the place. One evening he was feeling lonely and dissatisfied with all he had done. Somehow he felt compelled to go back to the wharf. He took his easel and his paints with him, even though he had painted there all day with little success. It was a beautiful moonlit night and the wharf was covered with mysterious shadows. Here was the picture Gutzon had been trying so hard to find. In a short time he completed the painting. He called it "Moonlight"

"Horse Thief," one of Borglum's early paintings

and when he took it to Keith for criticism, Keith remarked that it showed "true artistic feeling."

Not all Gutzon's work, however, met with such favor. One day at the Art Association, Williams was particularly critical. "You are in too much of a hurry," he said to Gutzon. "Why can't you take time to perfect one picture before you start another?" Gutzon was quite serious when he replied, "I must hurry. I have resolved to be great at thirty. So you see, I have no time to lose."

A lady, considerably over thirty, who had recently joined the class, overheard the conversation. When class was over she came to Gutzon and asked if she might look at his picture. "Go ahead," was the grumpy reply.

"I wonder who she is," thought Gutzon. And as if he had spoken aloud, she said, "My name is Elizabeth Putnam and I see by the signature on the picture you are J. G. Borglum." Already Gutzon was sorry he had been so abrupt with her. "My name is John Gutzon. Mostly I've been called Gutzon." Then he added, rather shyly, "One friend calls me Borgie. You are very kind to want to look at my painting, Miss Putnam."

"I've done a little teaching and I thought I might be able to help," she responded. Then she added, "I am Mrs. Putnam —a widow."

Gutzon watched her impatiently while she looked at his painting. He looked at her smooth dark hair and her clear, olive skin. "She is pretty," he thought.

He had begun to think she wasn't going to make any comment at all when she turned to him and said, rather gently, "If you work hard, you probably will be great at thirty."

After that, Gutzon and Martin, too, often sought Mrs. Putnam's advice. She herself painted mostly still life but she seemed to have a feeling for color. No matter what comments she made about their work, they always came away from her feeling that they were the best artists in the world.

By the time Gutzon had finished his course at the Art Association, he was calling Mrs. Putnam Lisa. She called him Zeno, a nickname she had given him. When Gutzon was ready to go back to Los Angeles, she promised that she would consider moving her studio there.

In Los Angeles, Gutzon moved his class outdoors for sketching. "Every artist," he told them, "must approach nature with great reverence."

He began work on the stage coach picture that had been in his mind since his train journey to San Francisco. The picture was on a canvas five feet by nine feet. The coach in the picture was to be drawn by six horses. Gutzon realized that if he were to paint lively, spirited horses, he would have to have fine models. He knew that the finest horses in southern California were to be found a few miles from Los Angeles on millionaire "Lucky" Baldwin's ranch. It never occurred to Gutzon that Baldwin might object to having his horses "sketched" by a young, unknown artist. It didn't even occur to him to make an appointment with the famous rancher. He simply took his easel and paints and went to the ranch.

Fortunately Baldwin had as much admiration for spirited young men as for spirited horses. "Go ahead," he said to Gutzon, "paint all you want. Paint me a couple of pictures, too." Gutzon considered this a commission and he wasted no time in painting portraits of two of the most famous of the Baldwin horses, Emperor Norfolk and Rey El Santa Anita. The rancher was so pleased with Gutzon's work that he urged him to spend as much time at the ranch as he wished. Gutzon loved being with the horses. Once he took his entire class of art students to the ranch and had them all painting horses. Sometimes he rode instead of painting. As a result, months passed, and the huge stage coach picture was still not nearly finished.

One morning he was alone in his studio at work on the stage coach canvas when there was a gentle knock at his door. Before he could say anything the door opened. Gutzon's first thought when he saw his visitor was, "I have never before seen such snowy white hair."

"I am Jessie Benton Frémont," she said. "I saw some of your paintings at Sanborn-Vail's picture frame shop and I thought I'd like to see more."

Gutzon was plainly delighted. She was the most distinguished guest he had had and he was brimming with enthusiasm as he showed her his horse pictures. Even though his "Staging in California" was not quite finished, Mrs. Frémont was visibly impressed. When she saw it, she exclaimed, "You will ride to fame on horseback!"

Mrs. Frémont asked if she could bring General Frémont the next day to sit for a portrait. Gutzon made no attempt to conceal his joy. Mrs. Frémont, despite her white hair, had a warm, youthful smile and her keen eyes sparkled with pleasure at Gutzon's happiness. "We'll be here then at two-thirty tomorrow afternoon," she said as she left.

Gutzon was much too excited to settle down to any more painting that day. Besides, he wanted to get a letter off to Lisa right away to tell her his good news. Mrs. Putnam and Gutzon had kept up a steady correspondence since Gutzon's return from San Francisco, but only now did Gutzon realize just how important this exchange of letters was to him. "I wish you were here right now," he wrote. "I have no fear but that I can do the portrait, but your presence would give me added confidence."

He spent the remainder of the day rigging a large canvas to an easel and getting his paints in order. He even made an attempt to tidy up the place by putting out of sight a number of chunks of clay. Recently he had been trying his hand at modeling.

Next afternoon, promptly at two-thirty, Mrs. Frémont came with the General. The gray, aging soldier and statesman leaned on his wife's arm. But when the General donned his military coat with the gold-fringed epaulets, he seemed to straighten his shoulders a bit and his deep-set blue eyes had a glint of fire and determination.

Mrs. Frémont seemed anxious to have the portrait completed as quickly as possible and so they came several times each week. Each time, when Gutzon began to paint, Mrs. Frémont would draw her chair up behind him, put her feet on the rounds of his chair, and watch every brush stroke.

Gutzon was really sorry to see the portrait nearing completion. He had grown fond of the Frémonts and looked forward to their visits. On the day when he was getting ready for the final sitting, instead of feeling elated because he had been able to please them both, he felt gloomy and sad. He was so deep in his thoughts that he didn't hear the door open and he was taken completely by surprise when he looked up and saw Lisa standing in the room.

Before she had time to say a word Gutzon had leaped up and kissed her first on one cheek and then on the other, much as one French dignitary might greet another. Then they both started laughing and talking at once. Lisa said she had been feeling gloomy, too. Many of her friends in San Francisco, including Gutzon's friend Martin Borgord, had gone to France to study. She could not afford to do that, but wanted a change of scenery, at least, so she had decided to move to Los Angeles.

"Staging in California," an early painting by Borglum

Of course, Lisa had scarcely caught her breath before Gutzon was asking her opinion of the Frémont portrait. She was obviously pleased with the picture, but it was "Staging in California" that caused her to exclaim, "You may even be great before you are thirty."

There was such an air of festivity about the studio when the Frémonts arrived that when Mrs. Frémont was introduced to Lisa, she said, "You must be good for Mr. Borglum. I have never seen him in such high good spirits before."

At the end of the afternoon Gutzon announced that he had completely finished the portrait. The General seemed quite pleased and readily gave his permission to allow the portrait to be exhibited for a time at an art gallery. "It is the most truthful portrait we have had," said Mrs. Frémont as they were leaving, "and I shall see that others know of your work."

Mrs. Frémont kept her word. She had a wide circle of friends and she saw to it that the General's portrait was viewed by all of them. She never lost an opportunity to send visitors from the East to Gutzon's studio.

Meanwhile Gutzon and Lisa were almost constant companions. So far she had not been able to find a studio. Gutzon had many pupils and it seemed quite natural for Lisa to attend the classes and help out. She had a sweet, friendly way about her and all the students liked her. Gutzon found he was depending on her more and more. It was the first time he had ever had anyone share his problems.

This was the first time, too, Gutzon had had a lady show concern about his welfare. He had grown up so fast he hadn't had time to bother about girl friends. He was twenty-two years old. Lisa was forty. But they shared the same interests and ambitions and when Gutzon suggested that they get married and open a studio together, the difference in their ages seemed of little importance to either of them.

They were married without fanfare by a Justice of the Peace. Afterwards Gutzon wrote one of his infrequent letters to his father and said, "I have just married the kindest woman in the world."

The Old World Beckons

3

ANY AMBITIONS Lisa may have had for herself apparently vanished when she became Mrs. J. G. Borglum. It was only because Gutzon insisted that she allowed her pictures of luscious fruits and flowers to hang side by side with his in their new studio on Second Street in the heart of the business district. Lisa seemed quite content to take over almost entirely the teaching of the art students to give Gutzon more and more time to paint. She also encouraged Gutzon to experiment with modeling in clay.

There was a little apartment connected with the studio and Lisa saw to it that Gutzon had hot meals, clean shirts, and pressed trousers. Gutzon enjoyed the food, but frankly admitted he didn't care much whether his clothes were pressed or not.

Mrs. Frémont sent dozens of people to the studio and occasionally somebody bought a picture. If it happened to be a wealthy visitor from the East, Mrs. Frémont often dropped the Borglums a note of advice ahead of the visit. Once when she was sending a group of New Yorkers, she wrote to Lisa, "If they ask, name $150 for the trees. And have Mr. Borglum tell them, as he told me, that he had the General and myself in mind when he painted them." She closed her note, "Trust me and mind me."

Mrs. Frémont felt that Gutzon could profit from study in France. At first Gutzon wasn't much interested. "It's time America established her own standard of art," contended Gutzon, "without always having to look to the Old World for guidance." It was actually the enthusiastic letters from Martin Borgord concerning his studies in France at the Beaux Arts and at the Julien Academy that finally convinced Gutzon of the value of study abroad. Once the idea caught fire in his mind, he was impatient to be on his way and, had it not been for Lisa, he probably would have simply closed the studio door and gone.

Lisa was more practical. "You know, Zeno," she said, "it will take money to live in France, and we barely have enough to get there. I think we should wait until we have saved more money." Gutzon frankly couldn't understand such an attitude. "We will worry about money when we get there," he said. And Lisa saw that he meant it.

Fortunately a couple of art-collecting friends of Mrs. Frémont who happened also to be lovers of horses visited Los Angeles and paid good prices for paintings made at the Baldwin ranch. It was Mrs. Frémont's suggestion that on his way east Gutzon have an exhibit of his work in Omaha. Together, Gutzon and Lisa had forty-three paintings. Mrs. Frémont also loaned them the painting of the General to include with their collection. "He is well known enough to draw a crowd," she said to Gutzon, "even if, as yet, you are not."

On the last day of May, 1890, Gutzon and Lisa stepped off the train in Omaha on the first lap of their journey to France. The entire Borglum clan turned out to meet them. Even though Gutzon had sent his father a sketch of himself with his newly grown mustache and goatee, his father was surprised when he saw him. "You have changed," he said. "You look like a real artist!"

Gutzon's stepmother also seemed genuinely glad to welcome him and Lisa. If Gutzon gave any thought to times past and taunts of "you'll never amount to anything," he gave no indication. He seemed quite content to enjoy the role of favorite son.

Mrs. Frémont had eased Gutzon's way by writing letters to E. Rosewater, the editor of the Omaha Bee and to George W. Lininger, prominent local art collector. Gutzon was elated when Lininger, whose art gallery adjoined his house in a fashionable section of the city, offered to hold a special showing of the Borglums' collection of paintings.

The show opened on Saturday, June 7, and that same day the Bee carried a lengthy story under the heading: "Mr. Borglum's Gems. The Great Works of an Artist in Whom Omaha has an Interest." The story proclaimed the huge "Staging in California" a "masterpiece." It also mentioned that Lisa's "studies of California grapes excels anything along that line that has been shown in Omaha." The article concluded with, "In all his work the artist shows such true artistic feeling that one can but predict a great future for him."

The show was such a success that Lininger bought many of the pictures himself. Years later J. L. Brandeis, owner of a large department store in Omaha, purchased the "Staging" picture from the Lininger estate. The picture hung in a prominent spot in the store for many years until it was presented to the Joslyn Art Museum in Omaha where it may be viewed today.

Gutzon and Lisa were entertained quite royally in Omaha and Gutzon so thoroughly enjoyed the attention he received that they extended their visit into July. When they did leave they had only the Frémont portrait and a few unsold paintings, and enough money to live for many months in France. They also had letters of introduction from Mrs. Frémont to several influential New Yorkers, including Collis P. Huntington, the railroad magnate, and young Theodore Roosevelt, who was then serving as a member of the United States Civil Service Commission under President Benjamin Harrison.

The Borglums stopped over in Chicago where Gutzon, on Mrs. Frémont's recommendation, had a commission to paint a portrait of a friend of hers named George Shoenberger. While they were in Chicago word reached them of the sudden death of General Frémont in New York City. Gutzon, of course, wrote Mrs. Frémont at once and when he got to New York there was a letter from her saying, "If you can spare the portrait of the General, I would be thankful to have it."

Despite the fact that Gutzon was getting restless and was eager to sail for Europe, he kept his promise to Mrs. Frémont and called on Huntington, Roosevelt, Philip Rollins, a wealthy businessman, and Henry Brace, an art connoisseur and authority in water colors, showing the General's portrait to all of them, before he sent it back to California.

As the SS Bourgogne sailed out of New York harbor, Gutzon waved cheerfully to the Statue of Liberty. "It's hard to believe she has only been there four years," said Gutzon. "She looks as if she had always been there."

"I'm sure she will be here to greet us when we come back," responded Lisa matter-of-factly. "Auguste Bartholdi, the sculptor, said he built her to last forever."

"It must be a wonderful feeling to create something that will last an eternity," said Gutzon. "But even more wonderful is it to be able to create such a magnificent symbol of American freedom. If a Frenchman can do that for our great country, I wonder why an American sculptor doesn't dream up a monument colossal enough to memorialize our belief in the right of every man to be free and happy."

"If you were a sculptor instead of a painter, you could do it," said Lisa teasingly.

Lisa and Gutzon had a happy time aboard ship. It was the first time since their marriage that they had had time to relax. They spent lazy hours planning a house among the orange groves of Southern California.

In Paris they had a wonderful reunion with their good friend, Martin Borgord. He had located a small studio apartment for them at 65 Boulevard Arago. It was a bit dingy and had a funny old stove with an isinglass door, but the rent was low and that was important.

They soon discovered that it was easiest to get around in Paris on a bicycle. Those first weeks when they bicycled together, getting acquainted with Paris, were, as Lisa wrote to Mrs. Frémont, "like living a storybook life." It was all just as they had pictured it—the book stalls along the River Seine, Notre Dame Cathedral, the tree-lined avenues on which artists painted, in their smocks and berets, and the wonderful museums and art galleries. "There is enough to keep a man here a lifetime," said Gutzon, "and still not see it all."

Through Borgord Gutzon was introduced to the Julien Academy and he lost no time in beginning his studies. Several of his masters encouraged him to try his hand at sculpturing and under their able tutelage Gutzon began to have more and more confidence in his ability as a sculptor.

Gutzon was so engrossed in his painting and sculpturing that he paid scant attention to the affairs of the house. He was quite content to have Lisa take over the job of stretching their meager finances.

Mrs. Frémont was fully aware of their financial difficulties. In fact she wrote, "I will do all in my power to keep you studying in Europe." It was she who sent word to Gutzon that Senator and Mrs. Leland Stanford were touring Europe and suggested that he make an effort to see them when they visited Paris. Gutzon followed her advice and Senator Stanford was so impressed with Gutzon and his work that he placed an order for three paintings. Lisa suspected Mrs. Frémont had written the Senator, too, because he made a substantial advance payment on the first painting. Unfortunately Gutzon completed only one of the paintings before Stanford's death. It was the only one for which he was paid. He later completed the others and petitioned the Stanford estate for payment but his request was denied because he had no written contract.

Philip Rollins, whom Gutzon had met in New York City, also visited Paris and sat for a portrait.

Despite his painting commissions, Gutzon became more and more interested in sculpturing. One day one of the masters at the Academy offered to take him to the state studio of Auguste Rodin near the University. These studios had been established by Louis IV, and sculptors who engaged in any public works were allowed the use of them without charge. Rodin, at fifty-one, with "The Thinker" yet to come, was struggling for recognition. His works were considered curiosities by many critics of the day. Rodin was extremely sensitive to the pulse of others, and must have sensed the creative longing in Gutzon, because he invited him to come back. Gutzon did go back again and again.

While Gutzon studied the basic techniques of sculpturing

at the Academy, it was in Rodin's studio that he learned the fundamental lessons of honesty in art. "In making a bust," advised Rodin, "you must create what you see, not what your model wishes you to see." He reaffirmed what Gutzon had always believed, that to be a great artist one should have respect for the beauty of nature.

Rodin's studio was littered with half-finished sketches and drawings. Once he saw Gutzon admiring a watercolor and he promptly scrawled on it, "To my friend, Borglum," signed his name, and presented it to Gutzon.

While Rodin scorned the opinions of the academicians, Gutzon yearned for some sign of official recognition of his abilities. He was anxious to have his work accepted for showing at the national art exhibit known as the Salon. He hoped also, before he left France, to have something accepted by the new Salon, and to become a member of the National Society of Beaux Arts. During the winter months Gutzon worked tirelessly to perfect a painting and a piece of sculpture that might win acceptance at the Salon.

Both Lisa and Gutzon, accustomed to the warm California winters, suffered with the cold. Gutzon complained that his hands were always cold. Fuel for the little stove was scarce. One raw, icy day when Borgord came home with Gutzon for dinner, Lisa delighted them both by coloring the isinglass in the stove door red and burning a candle inside. The flickering flame gave out a nice rosy glow and the three of them laughed and joked the entire evening and declared they had never been so warm.

Other young artists shook their heads dubiously when they saw what Gutzon was planning to submit to the Salon. The painting was of a tired, thin mare standing over her newborn colt. In the offing were three hungry looking wolves.

The painting by Borglum that was accepted by the Salon in
Paris (now owned by a collector in California)

The moon cast a weird light over the prairie scene. The little
piece of sculpture, too, was typically American. It was a horse
standing over a dead Indian. Gutzon was not perturbed by
his friends' uncertainty. He was an American and he wanted
his works to show it.

He was quite chagrined a few days later when he was
notified that his painting had been accepted but no mention
was made of the bronze. Then, a day or so after that, much
to his amazement, he received word that the bronze had been
accepted by the new Salon and that he was now a member
of the National Society of Beaux Arts. Evidently the delivery-
man had mistakenly delivered the bronze to the new Salon.
Gutzon was so afraid the whole thing was a mistake that he
didn't even acknowledge the membership. Only when he
received a personal letter of congratulation from the cele-

brated painter, Puvis de Chavannes, president of the new Salon, was he certain enough of his good fortune to write the news to his father and to Mrs. Frémont.

By March 25, 1891, his twenty-fourth birthday, Gutzon had completed six months' study at Julien Academy and had been accepted as a student at the Beaux Arts school. Also, an art dealer had sold several small paintings for him and for Lisa. "It's time we had a bit of a celebration," said Lisa. "I have already selected a birthday present for you, but you have to come with me to select the exact one you want."

Gutzon was as excited as a child. Lisa took him directly to a fancy pet store on the Champs Elysée and led him to a large cage in the corner. Two Great Dane puppies gazed longingly at Gutzon. "I couldn't decide which one to give you," said Lisa. "So I brought you to choose for yourself." Gutzon couldn't decide either and in the end they took both dogs.

Lisa had known all the time that even one dog would tax her rigid budget, but as the days passed, and she saw the great affection Gutzon had for his two dogs and the joy they gave him, she was glad that, for once, she had not been, as Borgord jokingly called her, "Gutzon's sensible half."

The Borglums had originally planned to return to California in the fall of 1891, but they had sold enough pictures to make it possible for them to pay a brief visit to Spain. They were both deeply interested in the old missions and in the Spanish background of California. When they confided their plans to Mrs. Frémont, she, as usual, came forth with some letters of introduction. One letter was to the American Minister to Spain, who, she said "had the misfortune to have the name of E. Burd Grubb. No matter his name," she went on, "he will be a pass key for you to the best thing you may wish to study."

The Borglum's "brief" visit to Spain lasted over a year. "There are but few Americans living in Spain," Lisa wrote to Mrs. Frémont, "but everywhere we go we are welcomed with sincere warmth."

In Madrid, Gutzon returned again and again to the bull-fights, even though the sight sickened him, to try to capture some of the excitement on canvas. He and Lisa visited dozens of cathedrals. Gutzon spent three months in Toledo painting a portrait of Don Tomas, the priest in charge of the great Gothic cathedral there. The Borglums reread Washington Irving's *Alhambra* and then went to Granada to visit the magnificent Moorish fortress. They spent weeks in museums studying the works of El Greco, Velazquez, Murillo, Goya, and other famous Spanish artists.

In a letter to his father, dated Christmas, 1892, Gutzon wrote, "You may expect to see us in Omaha after the New Year. I have in mind doing a great painting of Cortez' conquest in Mexico and I am anxious to go to California and get started." Then he added a postscript, "We bought ourselves two more Great Danes for Christmas, so counting me, there will be five Great Danes visiting you."

"Finis," a sketch of a bullfight done by Borglum in Spain

Actually it was the middle of February by the time Lisa, Gutzon, a Spanish servant, and the four dogs reached Omaha. Miller and Solon, who were operating a ranch in the western part of the state, both came home for the big event. In the eyes of his family, Gutzon was a tremendous success. But it was Solon who plied him with questions about his art studies in Europe and then rather timidly showed him some drawings he had made of horses and cattle on scraps of wrapping paper. Gutzon was frankly amazed at the photographic accuracy of Solon's sketches. He urged Solon to give up the ranch and come with him to California to study art. Solon was pleased, but he was not as impulsive as Gutzon, and he promised to give serious consideration to the offer.

Gutzon enjoyed the attention that was showered on him in Omaha, but, as usual, after a few days of inactivity, he grew restless. He was anxious to get settled in California and start on his painting. The family seemed genuinely sorry to see him leave. Lisa and Gutzon stood on the open platform of the observation coach and waved until they were out of sight. "I really had a good time at home, Lisa," said Gutzon. Then as an afterthought, he added, "I don't even mind calling Ida 'mama' any more."

The London Years

4

Mrs. Frémont, who was comfortably settled in a neat little cottage that had been presented to her by the women of Los Angeles, warmly welcomed the Borglums and their dogs. She offered them shelter at her Retreat, as she had named her house, until they could find a place to live.

It took the Borglums but a short while to decide that Los Angeles, with its miles of newly paved streets, cable and electric street cars, and new theaters, hotels, stores, and business houses of every description, had grown too citified for their liking. So they made a down payment on a house in the sleepy little village of Sierra Madre, a few miles from Los Angeles and close to the fine horses that Gutzon loved to paint and ride on the "Lucky" Baldwin ranch. The area abounded in orange and lemon trees, grapevines, and luxurious flowers. "There is enough beauty in nature here to keep me painting a lifetime," said Gutzon.

As soon as they were settled, Gutzon began serious work on his Cortez painting. When his friend Charles Lummis, who was now editor of *Land of Sunshine*, saw the canvas, he wrote: "It's a heroic painting of that most romantic episode in all the history of the Americas, the 'Noche Triste.' This great picture of that gray dawn on the broken causeway of Mexico, with the soldiers of Cortez floundering across the gap, beset by the Aztecs, is not yet finished, but it stands far enough to show composition that may properly be termed great."

Gutzon wrote glowing accounts to Solon of the life of an artist in California. Solon, who had given up ranching shortly after Gutzon's visit and returned to Omaha to study art under Rothery finally yielded to Gutzon's pleas to "come West where the opportunity is." Solon was particularly delighted with the magnificent horses at Baldwin's ranch and while he made literally hundreds of sketches of the horses, his real interest lay in the art of sculpturing. He stayed with Gutzon until he felt he knew enough to go out on his own. Then he rented a studio at Santa Ana for two dollars a month, hung a sign on his door that read "Studio Open on Saturdays Only," and soon had all the pupils he could handle in one day. Other days he worked on perfecting his sculpturing and studying nature by wandering about in the mountains.

Gutzon also became more and more interested in sculpturing and in 1894 he modeled a bust of the seventy-year-old Mrs. Frémont. Not only Mrs. Frémont, but Lily, her daughter, who was with her at the time, were well pleased with what they termed the "warmth" of the portrait.

Lisa tried to encourage Gutzon to finish his "Noche Triste" painting before he went on to other work. Already, however, Gutzon was growing weary of the quiet life in the country. When Lummis asked him to try his hand at writing an article for his magazine, Gutzon jumped at the chance. "But Zeno," protested Lisa, "you are an artist, not a writer." "From now on," answered Gutzon, "I am both." His article on California artists which appeared in the Spring of 1895 was the first of hundreds of magazine and newspaper articles to come from Gutzon's pen.

When Lummis wanted a new cover design for his magazine, he naturally turned to Gutzon, who was happy to add commercial art to his list of accomplishments. Gutzon designed a mountain lion, his head framed with a golden sun.

For a time Gutzon also worked with Lummis on plans for the restoration of California missions. However, since Gutzon had been to Spain, he felt he knew more about missions than Lummis possibly could. Lummis, who had founded the Landmarks Club, whose purpose was the preservation of missions and other historic relics, naturally felt he was an authority on

Bust of Jessie Benton Frémont by Borglum

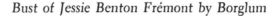

the methods of restoration. Despite the fact that the two friends quarreled bitterly over procedure, Gutzon did spend considerable time at the mission of San Juan Capistrano digging among the ruins and making suggestions to Lummis. He also painted a number of pictures of the old mission.

Gutzon was busy all the time, and yet he had to borrow money from friends to make ends meet. He had moved to Sierra Madre to have peace and quiet, but, as Lisa said one day to Mrs. Frémont, "Gutzon only wants peace and quiet when it's cluttered with guests and activity." Gutzon grew even more restless when Solon left to go to art school in Cincinnati.

Shortly before Thanksgiving in 1894 some malicious crank poisoned the four Great Danes and they died. After that Gutzon talked only of leaving California. Lisa was not at all happy about moving but when Gutzon made up his mind to go to England, she knew there was no point in protesting.

In the Spring of 1896, again armed with a stack of letters from Mrs. Frémont to influential friends in New York and in England, and a pile of unsold paintings, they started for England. They left the house in Sierra Madre in charge of their Spanish servant.

From the moment they arrived in London, Lisa was unhappy. She was nearing fifty and was tired of moving around. She still had great faith in Gutzon's ability as an artist, but his complete lack of regard for money was a constant worry to her. Gutzon had even borrowed funds from a wealthy cousin of Lisa to make the trip, and, despite their financial difficulties, had insisted on renting a rather spacious studio on Kensington High Street.

But Lisa was, temporarily at least, somewhat mollified when members of British royalty began to take notice of

Gutzon's paintings. One of the visitors to Gutzon's studio, a lady named Helene Bricka, was so delighted with his paintings that she arranged for several of the pictures to be shown to Queen Victoria at Osborne House. Lisa rejoiced with Gutzon when he received a letter from Lord Edward Clinton, master of the Osborne household, saying, "I am desired by the Queen to inform you that Her Majesty was very much pleased with your pictures that you were good enough to send her for Her Majesty's inspection."

When Mrs. Frémont received word of the attention Gutzon's work was receiving, she wrote, "Your darkest hour ends in a dawn of such real promise. I see now it is only a question of holding on. The English kindle slowly but burn steadily. Trust them and remain with them."

So long as people kept coming to view his work, Gutzon was encouraged, but this was not enough for Lisa. Finally, on the pretext of having to look after business matters concerning the house at Sierra Madre, Lisa went back to the States. At the last minute she tried to get Gutzon to come too, but he said, "I know I am on the threshold of success. Don't you recall, Lisa, telling me I would be great at thirty? I have not yet passed thirty so don't give up hope."

Whatever hope Gutzon may have held for real success at thirty died before the year was finished. Alone, discouraged, beset with debts, he hardly knew which way to turn. Yet he wrote to Lisa, "I feel it. I know the English are about to 'kindle.' Give me a little more time."

Gutzon received some inspiration from his association with the young artist, Frank Brangwyn, who, with his wife, lived in a Kensington flat. Brangwyn, after a long period of struggle, had finally established quite a reputation among art collectors. But he confided to Gutzon, "I make my living

Gutzon Borglum in his London studio

drawing sketches for magazines, not from the paintings I sell. I expect to furnish my home by exchanging paintings for pieces of furniture." Gutzon must have taken Brangwyn's experiences to heart because in November of 1897, he secured a piano in return for sketches to be "made from time to time" for a weekly magazine known as the *London Musical Courier*.

Small commissions began coming to Gutzon, too. His works were accepted for exhibit at the Royal Academy of Arts and a short while later he was made a member of the Royal Society of British Artists. Never once had Gutzon lost faith in his own ability. He never ceased to welcome with genuine warmth all visitors to his studio and one day he was rewarded. An official of the Midland Railway Company, William Towle, came, liked what he saw, and offered Gutzon a generous contract to do a series of large panels for the Queen's Hotel in Leeds.

Gutzon was overjoyed. He hastened to write the good news to Lisa and to his father but it was to Mrs. Frémont that he spoke his true feelings, "It is the first order of this kind I have ever enjoyed. It is epic making in my life. It is the turning point not only in my fortunes but in my art."

Gutzon had frequently remarked that he never looked back, only ahead. In the excitement of this fine commission, he found it easy to forget debts and past hardships. In fact the first thing he did was to rent a suburban villa, known as Harlestone. The villa, which was located at St. John's Wood, was surrounded by a beautiful garden. Before he moved in, Gutzon had elaborate alterations and repairs made on the property.

Then he began work on the Leeds panels which were to portray the four seasons of the year. Gutzon was allowed free rein to design and paint as he wished. Critics were frankly amazed at the delicate character of these paintings from the hand of an artist accustomed to producing bold western scenes. In each panel were graceful maidens with an expressive Pan, who changed from a sweet young child of nature in the spring panel to an old and gray winter Pan in the last panel.

The panels won for Gutzon the recognition he needed to "kindle" the British. Commissions for portraits and busts came pouring in. His portrait of Ned, son of Lord and Lady Latham, was exhibited at Macmillans on Bond Street, and opened a new field for Gutzon—portraiture of children. He was soon overwhelmed with commissions to paint children.

Gutzon thoroughly enjoyed the days he spent at various baronial country estates, sometimes doing several children's portraits in one family. On more than one occasion he remarked when he left a particularly lovable child, "I wish I could take you with me." Although Gutzon never discussed his home life with anyone, close friends were aware that he felt keenly the absence of children of his own.

One child, whose identity today remains a mystery, seems to have held a very special place in Gutzon's heart. Her name was Phyllis, and as far back as any of Gutzon's family can remember, the exquisite marble head of Phyllis served as a centerpiece on the big round Borglum table. If there were special guests, Phyllis might be surrounded with a garland of greens or flowers, but she was always there.

Gutzon's letters to Lisa gave every indication that he was meeting with success. Even so, when he did not urge her to return to England, she hoped he would soon tire of living abroad and come home to California. As the months went by, Lisa regretted more and more that she had not stayed with

"*Phyllis*"

Gutzon. Finally she went back to England to be with him.

She found Gutzon in high spirits. He had just returned from a trip to Leeds to oversee the placing of his panels. During his stay at Leeds he had met his friend Roberts, a musician who not only played but made organs. Roberts was on his way to visit the ailing John Ruskin at Brantwood, his home on Coniston Lake, and invited Gutzon to go along. While Roberts and Ruskin talked about organs, Gutzon filled his sketchbook with drawings of the great man. "As soon as I have time," Gutzon told Lisa, "I will make a statue of Ruskin."

Lisa was disappointed to find that Gutzon had little time for relaxing. In fact there were not enough hours in the day for him to do all the things he had to do. He was still "paying" for his piano, and now for several other pieces of furniture, by drawing advertisements for magazines. Harlestone Villa seemed always in need of repair and demanded a great deal of Gutzon's time. As a member of the Royal Society of British

Artists, Gutzon spent considerable time planning his work for exhibition at the Society showings.

When the Boer War broke out, Gutzon immediately went to work for an English periodical, *Black and White*, drawing maps and pictures of war scenes. He was so inspired by the drama of the war that he modeled a small bronze of a figure of a depressed looking Boer general on a dejected horse. At the time the bronze was publicly shown in England, it was acclaimed by a French art critic as "one of the most beautiful things in the exhibition."

During this period Gutzon also created a little bronze of two young Indians in desperate flight on horseback which he called "Pursued." The statue was purchased by Emperor Wilhelm II of Germany.

Meantime, Solon, who had won a scholarship in Cincinnati that had enabled him to study in Paris at Julien Academy, had already received honorable mention for western bronzes exhibited at the Salon. His brothers' success brought Auguste Borglum to England to pursue his studies in music. Auguste settled himself in a small apartment in London, but he spent much of his time with Gutzon and Lisa at Harlestone.

Gutzon was fond of giving big parties. Auguste, who wrote long, detailed letters home, described for his father one of the more spectacular gatherings. "There were many elegantly dressed ladies and gentlemen. They had come to see a talented young dancer from California named Isadora Duncan perform. I must say she was a real success. She danced barefooted with complete abandon but so beautifully that many of Gutzon's staid British guests engaged her right then and there to perform at various functions."

On several occasions Auguste and Gutzon visited Solon in Paris. However after Solon married Emma, a French girl,

Auguste went more often alone. He finally admitted that it was Emma's sister, Lucy, that drew him so often to Paris, so that it was no surprise to Gutzon when Auguste announced that he and Lucy were to be married.

While Gutzon and Solon always remained good friends, Solon's marriage seemed to create a barrier between them. Gutzon once wrote to a friend, "I seldom see Solon. His dear wife in her sweet French feminine simplicity prohibits his traveling at large."

At the turn of the century Gutzon had commissions enough to keep him busy for a year. Articles written by him on notable artists and their works were appearing regularly in *The Artist*, a fine British art magazine.

Still he was hounded with debt. Lisa tried very hard to work out some sort of financial budget, but Gutzon gave her no cooperation. Just when she counted on a particularly large sale to pay long past due rent and clear up overdue notes owed to friends, Gutzon in a magnanimous show of generosity, sent his stepmother and stepsister Harriett tickets for a vacation in England and Denmark. When they arrived, Gutzon had a wonderful time sightseeing with them and showing off his Villa. They left, thoroughly convinced that Gutzon had made a fortune. In truth, Gutzon at this point had written an old friend and art dealer, George Elliott, in Los Angeles, about sending watercolors to him for possible sale. Gutzon received the discouraging reply, "About the watercolors. I cannot encourage you to send them. As to prices, $25 is high and a $50 watercolor is something so swell that one buying such a picture would be looked upon as real devilish."

Gutzon hardly knew which way to turn. He was even overdrawn at his bank. "If I could just go away some place, maybe I could work things out," said Gutzon. So Lisa borrowed money for a vacation to Paris. Gutzon, in a nostalgic mood, suggested they rent an apartment in the same building where they had lived eleven years before. "It's a good omen," Gutzon told Lisa when they were fortunate enough to find a vacancy at 65 Boulevard Arago.

Gutzon was right about the good omen, because shortly after they were settled, he received word from the Midland Railway Company that they were contemplating building a new hotel at Manchester. They wanted to know if Gutzon would be interested in doing the decorations, and if so, would he be willing to go to America to study mural paintings and decorations in outstanding American hotels.

Gutzon was jubilant. "A trip to America is just what I need," he said. Lisa decided she would stay in Paris while Gutzon was gone. He sailed from Cherbourg on the Dutch steamer *Rynddam* on November 14, 1901. He had with him only a few clothes and a small selection of his paintings and bronzes to exhibit in the States. "I'll be back before Christmas," he assured Lisa.

Aboard ship Gutzon shed his problems. He entered into all the festivities and joined in the games. He especially enjoyed the company of Mary Montgomery, a young woman on her way home from the University of Berlin where she had just received her Ph.D. degree. She spoke half a dozen languages and no matter what Gutzon chose to argue about, she could hold her own. By the time the ship reached America, Gutzon was already calling her "Peggy," and she called him "Dane." In New York City they parted, promising to meet again soon. Mary was engaged to work with Dr. Henry Smith Williams, compiling material for the *Historian's History of the World*. She very generously offered to help Gutzon should he have need of a secretary during his stay in America.

Gutzon established himself at the Marlborough Hotel at Broadway and Thirty-sixth Street and began his inspection of murals. He honestly had every intention of returning to Paris by Christmas. Then he heard about a government competition: the selection of a sculptor for a monument honoring General Grant. "This is an opportunity too good to miss," Gutzon wrote Lisa. "The government has allotted two hundred and fifty thousand dollars for the work. Besides the money, this would establish me as a sculptor in America, if I could win. Solon is competing, too. If I don't win, I hope he does." Since the Manchester hotel was still in the planning stage, the Midland Railway people gladly gave Gutzon more time in the States.

Gutzon threw himself wholeheartedly into the work of designing the Grant memorial, as he did with every fresh project. This was the first large competition he had ever entered and for two months he thought of little else. "Maybe I had to have those years abroad to appreciate my own country," mused Gutzon. He had always been interested in the history of America but now he took time to delve deeply into the period of the Civil War. His finished model showed General Grant holding a spirited horse in check as he turns to address two mounted aids. All around the pedestal was a continuous series of reliefs telling the history of the War Between the States. Gutzon submitted his model on March 31, 1902, and when it was put on public display with the other models in the basement of the Corcoran Gallery of Art in Washington, D.C. the *Washington Evening Star* described it as one of the "finest works of sculpture and one of the most dignified compositions of all those shown."

Gutzon wrote to Lisa as well as to his dear friend Mrs. Frémont, "My model is so well received. I feel I have a good chance of winning the award. I will let you know as soon as I know the outcome. Meantime I will catch up on some rest. I am exhausted."

The letters had not had time to be delivered when Gutzon received a curt notice to remove his model on the ground that it was ineligible for the competition. Gutzon was stunned. In fact, so great was his disappointment that he became physically ill. How the decision was made to disqualify Gutzon's work is not really known, but Gutzon wrote in his memoirs: "Augustus Saint-Gaudens, who was acting in an advisory capacity to the Memorial Commission, insisted on the removal of my model on the ground that I had had help from a European sculptor, that nobody in America could produce a model of that kind."

Gutzon made other charges in his memoirs, too. He claimed that Solon, in addition to submitting a design of his own for the original competition, had been hired to model the horses in the designs submitted by Charles H. Niehaus and Massy Rind, who took second and third places. A young sculptor named Henry M. Shrady won first place. Shrady and Niehaus were then asked to compete again for the central figure in the monument. According to Gutzon, Shrady paid Solon $500 to design the horse for his model and then Niehaus called on Gutzon for help with his design. Gutzon wrote, "Of course I refused, but I didn't blame Solon for accepting. I blamed the sculptors who took advantage of artists who were in need of funds." Regardless of Gutzon's claims, one fact is certain. Shrady won the competition.

Gutzon never again entered a major competition for a monument, either public or private. Nor did he ever miss an opportunity to expound publicly on the evils of competition in art.

The Thirty-Eighth Street Studio

5

THE GRANT MEMORIAL COMPETITION made Gutzon realize how much he wanted recognition and respect from his fellow Americans. He was sorry he had stayed abroad so long.

There was another, more personal, reason for Gutzon's mental turmoil at this time. He had known for a long time that he was not happy living with Lisa. Each year the gap in their ages had seemed to grow wider. Gutzon wanted children. Lisa didn't. Gutzon wanted to be free to work and eat and sleep at any hour of the day. Lisa wanted a more conventional way of life. Gutzon was torn between his gratitude to Lisa for the help and encouragement she had given him and his desire to be free of her. He treated this problem as he did most disagreeable problems that confronted him. He tried to ignore it. Instead of writing Lisa that he did not intend to live abroad again, he let her assume that press of work in America was delaying him.

At this point, if he hadn't needed the money so badly, he probably would have given up painting and devoted his entire time to sculpturing. But the commission to do the Midland Railway paintings was too valuable to ignore and, in August 1902, he signed a contract to do the work. That same month, on the strength of the funds from the Midland work, he arranged to have the well-known architectural firm of George Lewis Heins and Christopher Grant La Farge prepare a studio for him from a remodeled stable behind a row of brownstone front houses. The studio was at 166 East Thirty-eighth Street in New York City.

He accepted Mary Montgomery's offer to help him with secretarial work. It seemed only natural then that he should consult her concerning problems that arose in connection with the remodeling of his studio and the two of them were together more and more. When Gutzon's stepsister Dot decided to visit New York, Gutzon called on Miss Montgomery to help entertain her and to select presents for him to send back to the family in Omaha.

Gutzon set up his easels and unpacked his paints with the carpenters and workmen still in the studio and began to design the murals for England. He arranged to make a hurried trip to London as soon as he completed the designs, to get them approved and to make some measurements for the placing of the finished pictures. But the strain of the past few months, backed by years of unrest and unhappiness, was too much for Gutzon and on September 4, 1902 he entered Miss Alston's Hospital on Sixty-first Street completely broken in spirit and in health. His illness was diagnosed as typhoid fever.

He refused to allow his family in Omaha to be informed of his illness but when, after weeks of hospital care, he grew steadily worse, Lisa was notified of his condition. She reached America with Jeanne, a French maid, in December, to find that much of the time Gutzon had been unconscious or delirious and that the typhoid fever had been followed by brain fever.

Two days after Christmas, while he was still in the hospital,

Gutzon's dear friend Jessie Benton Frémont died, but he was not told until much later.

Gutzon left the hospital pale, thin, and minus a good bit of his thick brown hair, but with a grim determination to begin life anew. Lisa refused to believe that Gutzon really wanted to divorce her. She finally agreed to a separation to give Gutzon more time to think things over, and she and Jeanne went to Sierra Madre. After she left, Gutzon wrote her a long letter confirming their financial agreement. He wrote, "I wish you would let me know how far this is as you wish it and if you can be comfortable by this arrangement." He signed his letter, "Yours affectionately."

While the arrangement with Lisa was only a temporary one, Gutzon felt they were on their way to an understanding, and he was gayer than he had been for years as he set about completing his studio. He began the transformation at the entrance to the old driveway on Thirty-eighth Street by painting the two big wooden gates a lovely shade of spring green. The driveway became a pathway bordered by flowers that led directly to the old barn which, with the help of the architects, had been cleverly converted into an immense studio with a skylight. At one end of the room was a balcony which Gutzon festooned with bright rugs and tapestries. Under the balcony was a low-ceilinged alcove with a big terra cotta fireplace, some built-in seats, and a grand piano.

By March Gutzon had fully recovered his health, his studio was in order, and he began serious work on the Midland hotel paintings. He was in a carefree mood. He knew that twenty-five thousand dollars awaited him on completion of the pictures. The first painting, which was ten feet high and twenty-six feet wide, depicted Sir Launcelot and Queen Guinevere riding on handsome horses through an English forest. They

One of Borglum's paintings for the Midland Hotel

were trailed by countless mounted men in armor. In addition, there were eleven large panels showing scenes from Shakespeare's *Midsummer Night's Dream*. He put on the last dab of paint on June 30th and the following morning he sailed with the canvasses to England.

Gutzon stayed in England only long enough to oversee the placing of his pictures and to collect his money. On his return to New York, he all but closed the door on his career as a painter and directed his creative talents toward the art of sculpturing.

Gutzon's studio was within walking distance of Grand

Central Station and relatives, friends, and friends of friends
who came to New York City made the studio their first stop.
Gutzon could talk and work at the same time and he seemed
to thrive on interruptions.

There was always a steady stream of admiring art students
to watch him work and he patiently answered all their questions. Occasionally he allowed students to work as studio
helpers and in return for their services he criticized their work.
These privileged students never forgot their experiences under
the tutelage of the warm, friendly "Borgie" as Gutzon was
often affectionately called. One such student, Marion Bell,
daughter of Alexander Graham Bell, remarked more than
fifty years after her experience that "working in Gutzon Borglum's studio was one of the high spots of my young life."

Young Marion and her good friend Alice Hill went up
from Washington, D.C. to work in the studio. Work meant
keeping damp the cloths that swathed the many clay figures
Gutzon was working on, mixing clay, and sometimes even
sweeping the floor. They didn't mind the work. It was a real
inspiration to them to watch Gutzon's strong, sure hands
fashion a drab glob of clay into a thing of beauty. Once
Marion got roundly scolded because she replaced some half-
wilted flowers on the fireplace with fresh ones. That's how
she learned that Gutzon liked the soft, faded colors of
withered plants.

The two girls roomed in a nearby boarding house and often
came back to the studio after dinner for hours of soul-inspiring
talk around a low-burning fire. Usually they were joined by
two young men whom Gutzon was trying to encourage and
help. One was Paul Nocquet, a talented Belgian artist, and
the other, a musician, Franklin Harris. The evenings usually
ended with "Harry" playing the piano and the two girls listen-

ing, dreamy-eyed. Alice and Franklin Harris fell in love and were married the following spring.

For Marion Bell, this marked the beginning of a lifelong friendship with Gutzon. No doubt Alexander Graham Bell was influenced somewhat by his daughter's enthusiasm for Gutzon's work when he asked him to submit plans for a Smithsonian monument. As a regent of the Smithsonian, Doctor Bell had gone to Genoa, Italy, in December, 1903, to arrange to transfer to America the remains of James Smithson, the English scientist who had bequeathed his fortune to the United States for the founding of the "Smithsonian Institution, an establishment for the increase and diffusion of knowledge among men."

The following July, Doctor Bell asked Gutzon to submit plans for a suitable Smithson memorial. Before he attempted to design a memorial to anyone, it was Gutzon's habit to

Borglum's statue of James Smithson

study the background of the person to be honored. Smithson was no exception. Gutzon spent weeks getting acquainted with the eccentric scientist.

Not until October did Gutzon have two elaborate plans in shape to send to Doctor Bell. One plan was a design for a special room for the tomb and the other was a plaster model of a statue of James Smithson which Borglum suggested placing directly on the walk leading from the front of the building. Doctor Bell paid Gutzon $586.10 for his plans, but there is no evidence that either of them was ever used. The statue that now stands in front of the Smithsonian is of Joseph Henry, the first secretary of the Institution. The model of the Smithson statue was widely exhibited and some critics called it "one of Borglum's best sculptural works." With the passing of the years, even the little model of Smithson has disappeared and only pictures remain as a record of its existence.

Also during the early 1900s, along with practically every other artist in America and many throughout the world, Gutzon was putting his whole heart into the preparation of exhibits for the World's Fair to be held in St. Louis in 1904.

Gutzon's pièce de résistance was a half circle of wild horses in a mad stampede. There was a lean, bony naked rider on the back of the lead horse, hanging on with one arm while the other arm seemed to be warding off the teeth of an oncoming horse.

At the time that Gutzon was working on this frantic group of horses, he was also putting the finishing touches on a tiny ferocious looking statue of Nero. The ill-tempered ten-inch Nero was almost frightening in his ugliness. Gutzon explained his creation of Nero by saying, "Each of us puts something of his life in his work. Something in my life made my Nero possible."

Gutzon also found time to model his Ruskin for St. Louis. He studied the sketches he had made when he visited the famous man and the result was a peaceful, sympathetic portrayal. The slumped, seated Ruskin is bundled up in a big rough coat, his knees covered with a throw. Even though his eyes and cheeks are sunken, Gutzon somehow managed to portray Ruskin's alertness and keenness of mind.

Gutzon usually had a name for his statues before he even started them, but he was ready to ship his statues to St. Louis and his group of horses was still unnamed. Gutzon had gotten the theme for the group from stories he had heard as a boy in the Middle West of the theft of range horses. He pictured an outlaw or an Indian leading a band of horses in a stampede. He said he took the clothes off the rider because they seemed cumbersome. He was about to label the bronze "Stampede"

"Mares of Diomedes," now in Metropolitan Museum of Art

Statue of Ruskin

when a visitor in his studio, unaware of the theme used for the statue, remarked, "What a magnificent portrayal of the horses of Diomedes!"

"You've just named the group," said Gutzon. From now on they are the "Mares of Diomedes." Whether the rider is fabled Diomedes, King of Thrace, about to be devoured by his own man-eating horses, or Hercules leading the horses after they have destroyed Diomedes, is left to the viewer to decide.

At St. Louis, Gutzon was awarded a gold medal for the "Mares of Diomedes." Mrs. Frémont's prediction that he would "ride to fame on horseback" was at last coming true.

The "Mares" was purchased by James Stillman, a wealthy New York banker, who presented it to the Metropolitan Museum of Art in New York City where it may be seen today. Later the bronze Ruskin was also acquired by the Metropolitan.

While he was making statues for the St. Louis exhibition, Gutzon also designed a series of fantastic gargoyles for the Class of 1879 dormitory at Princeton University. Gutzon later admitted that when he accepted the commission to do the gargoyles he had no idea how to begin. "I at length discovered," said Gutzon, "that the gargoyle was the expression of an ignorant, superstitious artisan who imagined the projections of buildings to be the spirits he feared and who fashioned them accordingly." Working on the premise that a gargoyle was merely a distortion of a natural thing, Gutzon, with his vivid imagination, had a wonderful time. He created North Wind, a wild-eyed creature with a distended nostril and a hideously curved mouth emitting the fury of a blast from the North. He named all the gargoyles. One, called Half-Equipped, was a bird with one arm, one leg, and one foot, but in spite of all, happy. Gutzon explained, "The half-equipped are always happy."

Since the Grant Memorial incident Gutzon had spoken out at every opportunity against competitions and against the lack of encouragement and opportunity given to young artists in America. No sooner had he been made a member of the National Sculpture Society than he proposed sweeping changes in the constitution which he said would make the group more democratic. The eminent sculptor, John Quincy Adams Ward, took this as a personal affront to his leadership as president of the organization and refused to give the report a hearing. In his anger, Gutzon ignored the fact that Ward was considered dean of the profession and had been president of the Society since its founding in 1893. He publicly proclaimed Ward unfair and discourteous. Ward seems to have remained aloof, as if he were above such petty quarrels.

This was only the first of many disputes Borglum had with various art associations that he considered unfair to young unknown artists. Nor did Gutzon's' reform ideas stop with art. He served for years on the Central Park Committee of the Metropolitan Parks Association in New York City and fought vigorously for better playgrounds for children and for more informality in public gardens. Newspapers soon discovered that Gutzon, always outspoken about anything he sincerely believed in, was good copy. Gutzon, on his part, thoroughly enjoyed publicity. Even bad publicity he took rather philosophically as part of the penalty for having the courage of his convictions. Never was he known to back down from a fight no matter whose side the press was on.

Gutzon's publicity was not confined to New York papers. In 1905 papers throughout the United States gave space to a most unusual controversy in which Gutzon was involved. Strangely enough, this controversy dealt with angels.

Early in the year Gutzon had been awarded the commission to model and supervise the carving of a host of saints and angels for Belmont Chapel, the first of seven chapels to be completed at the magnificent Cathedral of St. John the Divine in New York City. The romanesque cathedral, one of the largest in the United States, had been designed in 1891 by architects Heins and La Farge and the cornerstone was laid in 1892. Gutzon was proud to be associated with such a beautiful work and he was progressing quite happily until one day a visiting clergyman noted that two of the angels, Gabriel, the Angel of the Annunciation, and Michael, the Angel of the Resurrection, looked a little too feminine. Newspapers took

*Three Apostles, done by Borglum for the
Cathedral of St. John the Divine in New York*

up the criticism with almost fiendish delight. They carried
lengthy discussions on whether angels were masculine or feminine. Gutzon said, "I have read more about the angels than
any one single sane person has any business to. I have come to
the conclusion that the subject is one about which no one
really knows anything at all."

In answer to the criticism, he wrote to Dr. John Peters,
Canon of the Cathedral, "I shall change the angels as you sug-

gest." How he executed the change is not a matter of accurate record. Some newspapers claimed he smashed the two offending angels to bits and completely remade them. Other papers reported that he removed only the faces and substituted faces with a little less sweetness and tenderness. In any event, Gutzon himself thought the original Angel of the Annunciation was one of his finest works and he preserved the "feminine" mask and had it cast in silver.

Gutzon had other problems too with his divine characters. He discovered that instead of having carvers copy his models in marble, the contractor, in order to save money, was having the statues machine-cut in a stone yard. Gutzon was furious and, eventually, with the help of the press and sympathetic art critics, he won his point. He set up a studio on the Cathedral grounds and personally supervised the carving of every statue. For months Gutzon spent his mornings on scaffolding at the chapel recutting and finishing statues that had already been set in place against his will.

The last statue to be put in place was the one of Saint Andrew. Gutzon was in a gay mood as he watched Saint Andrew, swathed in heavy protective burlap, being hoisted slowly into place by a derrick. The statue was about halfway up when it suddenly began to slip and tumbled back to earth. Fortunately Saint Andrew landed in a pile of rubble and Gutzon found, to his great relief, when he tore off the burlap that the only damage was a fractured left arm and a few cuts. He was able to make the repairs quickly and easily. Despite the difficulties Gutzon and the churchmen were well pleased with the serenity and the beauty of the finished statues.

His many commissions and his activities in civic affairs kept Gutzon busy all the time. Still he was faced with the same old bothersome problem—not enough money. When he tried to recall what had happened to all the fees he had collected, he couldn't remember how much he had given his young stepbrother Francis to tide him and his family over for four months of post graduate work at a medical school. Nor had he made any record of a loan or two to his father or of the cost of stepsister Dora's Christmas vacation in New York for which he had paid. Lisa still refused to consent to a divorce and Gutzon was doing his best to support her at Sierra Madre.

Gutzon celebrated his thirty-ninth birthday on March 25, 1906, by writing some resolutions for the coming year. He underscored two of the resolutions: Number One—All obligations to friends of my youth of a money nature must be squared. Number Two—A home found and horses of my own.

Gutzon's "Pipe-Dream" Goes to Washington

6

OTHER ARTISTS in New York City may have had more elaborate studios than Gutzon, but certainly in 1906 none could boast more unusual decorations. Gutzon had recently joined the growing band of airplane enthusiasts and with his usual vigor was trying to learn all there was to know about flying machines. From the ceiling of his studio dangled dozens of models of different kinds of aircraft. Some, Gutzon had made himself. Other models belonged to members of the Aero Club of America who often came to the studio to discuss the latest aeronautical inventions.

Gutzon's young friend Paul Nocquet, one of the most frequent visitors, was especially enthusiastic about balloons. He was having the usual struggle of young artists to win recognition and told Gutzon that he liked to go up in a balloon because when he was up in the air he found it easy to relax and forget all his problems.

Nocquet must have been feeling especially discouraged when he made his balloon ascension in the late afternoon of April 4th. "I shall furnish you with a sensation," he remarked as he took off. The last time his balloon was seen it was drifting toward the sea. Next morning, after the tide receded, Nocquet's body was found lying face down in the soft marshes of Long Island. In his pocket was found a will which said, "In case of my death notify my good friend Borglum." Then he went on to give instructions concerning the sale of his works and the transfer of the money to his mother in Belgium. He ended his will with, "It was my ambition to become an American."

Gutzon was heartbroken. After the funeral, which was held in his studio, he arranged for a memorial exhibition of Nocquet's works at the American Art Galleries. The Honorary Committee for the showing was headed by President Theodore Roosevelt, whom Gutzon had met years before through an introduction from Mrs. Frémont, and included such luminaries as Frank Damrosch, Auguste Rodin, Augustus Saint-Gaudens, and even the actress Sarah Bernhardt. As a result of the exhibition, Nocquet's works were sold for good prices. "It's too bad," observed Gutzon sadly, "that poor Nocquet had to die before his works could be sold."

Nocquet's death may have influenced Gutzon to help young artists by teaching at the Art Student's League. He taught modeling from May until January without any pay. For the following five months he was paid one hundred dollars a month. While he taught at the League, he persuaded the Board of Control to make a number of improvements in the working conditions of the students, including the remodeling and painting of the modeling room and the building of shelves and installation of lockers. At the end of the time, Gutzon donated his earnings to be used as awards to students who showed the greatest progress, promise, and creative ability.

With all Gutzon's activities, he still found ample time for sculpturing. In addition to his work on commissions he permitted himself the "luxury," as he termed it, of creating pipe-dreams. These pipe-dreams often betrayed the tenderness and gentleness of Gutzon's character. One marble that he did purely for his own enjoyment was of a lovely woman gazing at a baby in her arms. He called this "The Wonderment of Motherhood."

Another work that gave Gutzon much pleasure was a tiny statuette of a dancer. Gutzon's friend, Isadora Duncan, who had danced in his London studio, had returned from Europe and had opened a little studio in New York. Gutzon called on her, watched her dance again, and was so inspired he fashioned a tiny, graceful, dancing figure. The statue was barely finished when a clumsy worker in the studio bumped against the pedestal and it fell to the floor. Gutzon ranted and raved and fired the workman. Then he picked up the broken bits of plaster. Head, arms, and legs were gone, but the dancing torso remained intact. Gutzon looked at it in amazement. "It is more beautiful this way," he said.

Years later, Isadora Duncan died a violent death. Her neck was broken when the end of a gorgeous red scarf she had wound about her shoulders caught in the wire spokes of a wheel of an open car in which she was riding. "The world has lost a great, creative dancer," said Gutzon sadly.

Gutzon never forgot Isadora Duncan. It is possible he was thinking of her many years later when he designed a statue of dancer Angna Enters. He molded Miss Enters headless, armless, and with one leg off at the knee and the other cut at the ankle. Long after that he presented a bronze headless, armless, and legless Dancer to the Corcoran Gallery of Art in Washington, D.C. But it remains a mystery whether this statue is modeled after Isadora Duncan or Angna Enters. Gutzon's letter to the Corcoran at the time of the presentation did not give the name of the model, but did state that the statue had once been complete and explained how it came to be broken. This would seem to indicate clearly that it was the one of Isadora Duncan, but it appears to be identical to the one of Miss Enters which never had head, arms, or legs, and Miss Enters herself believes the Corcoran statue is the one for which she was the model.

Sometimes commissions came to Gutzon from quite unexpected sources. One day he got a telephone call from Bob Davis, a man he hadn't heard from for almost twenty years. "I was an apprentice in a printshop near your studio on Fort Hill in Los Angeles," said Davis. "I used to drop in now and then and watch you work. In fact, I watched your portrait of General Frémont come to life and I never forgot it." Davis was now editor of the first ten-cent monthly to be published in America. It was called *Munsey's Magazine*. His brother, Sam, Nevada State Comptroller, was in town to discuss with Clarence Mackay, son of the famous chief of the bonanza kings, John W. Mackay, the possibility of a statue of his famous father.

A few days after this telephone conversation, Gutzon had the commission, had met young Mackay, and had arranged for a series of interviews with him to get background material on the life of the silver miner who became a millionaire. From Mackay's widow Gutzon secured the miner's clothes that the Big Bonanza King had worn the last time he went down into the sweltering mine to do manual labor. On June 25, 1906, Gutzon wrote to Clarence Mackay, "The statue of your father is now done. While a week ago it seemed to lack something, the last few days have given it a distinction I am very proud of."

Gutzon had modeled Mackay in a flannel shirt and clay-

Statue of
John W. Mackay
at entrance to
The Mackay School
of Mines

stained, crumpled trousers tucked into the tops of heavy
boots. In one hand he had a prospector's pick and in the
other a piece of ore. Clarence Mackay was pleased with the
statue of his father which, he said, "is marked by character-
istic energy and, considering you never knew my father, is
strikingly lifelike."

To make sure that his statue had a proper setting, Gutzon went to Nevada to select a site for it. First he went to
the capital, Carson City, but he couldn't find a single park
or city square that he felt was handsome enough to do justice
to Mackay. He visited several other cities with the same result. Then he went to Reno where he was warmly received
at the University of Nevada. He picked out a spot on the
campus and in a short time Sam Davis arranged for a dedication ceremony. Clarence Mackay decided that a new School

of Mines building would be a suitable background for his father's statue and he donated enough money to build it. The cornerstone for the new building was laid the same day the statue was dedicated. Later the Mackay clan decided that the University needed a few more buildings and before they were through they had given three. Gutzon came away from Nevada thoroughly imbued with the glamour and romance of the mining industry and with a part interest in a mine known as the Diamond Bullfrog. While the venture never made any money for Gutzon, he got much pleasure for years from talking about "my Diamond Bullfrog in Nevada."

Clarence Mackay was a satisfied customer and he never missed an opportunity to praise Gutzon. One of Mackay's friends was on a committee in Washington, D.C. charged with choosing a sculptor for a statue of General Philip H. Sheridan and Mackay recommended Gutzon for the work. For some years, the commission to make the statue had been in the hands of the aging J.Q.A. Ward, with whom Gutzon had tangled over Sculpture Society affairs, but Ward had not been able to please Mrs. Sheridan. The committee had finally given up on Ward and, according to Mackay, were ready to consider another artist.

Gutzon really wanted this commission, because it was an opportunity to place a statue in the nation's capital. Besides, $49,500 was to be paid for the statue and Gutzon, as always, needed money. He had recently bought his Thirty-eighth Street studio. It wasn't exactly what he had in mind for a "home" but it was a start. He had also purchased a thoroughbred Arabian horse named Halool. This, of course, had made it necessary for him to rent a stable. Gutzon had also hired a good-natured, slow-moving fellow named Sam Banks to help clean up around the stable and look after the horse.

As it turned out, Sam looked after Gutzon, too, and helped out in the studio.

Gutzon very carefully set about laying the groundwork for getting the Sheridan commission. He had missed out on Grant and he was determined not to miss out this time. First he read the life of Sheridan. Then, through a friend in Washington, he got himself invited to a dinner given by socialite Mrs. Herbert Wadsworth at which Sheridan's widow was also a guest. Before the evening was over Mrs. Sheridan had accepted Gutzon's invitation to visit his New York studio with her son, Lt. Philip Sheridan. "You seem to have such a deep respect for men who have served their country," Mrs. Sheridan said to Gutzon, "that I am sure you will make a good statue of the General."

Mrs. Sheridan must have been pleased with what she saw in the studio because on July 2, 1907 Col. Charles G. Bromwell, Executive Officer of the committee, asked Borglum to call at his office to work out a contract. He suggested that Gutzon "keep the matter confidential until the contract was actually signed." On July 31st, Secretary of War William Howard Taft, who was also on the committee, directed the award of the contract to Gutzon.

Gutzon, of course, was overjoyed. He studied carefully all the Civil War material he had collected when he had worked on Grant. He gave particular attention to clothes and equipment used and to the battles in which General Sheridan had been engaged. He visited Mrs. Sheridan many times to consult her about details of the General's life. Once he spent an entire day at the Sheridan home making sketches of the General's sword. He was in touch with many of Sheridan's associates, including Col. Royal E. Whitman. Gutzon went with Whitman to Governor's Island in New York City to view Sheridan's stuffed horse, Rienzi, but he said he couldn't use a dead thing for a model, so he bought a Virginia hunter named Smoke to serve as the model.

After weeks of study Gutzon decided to picture the five-foot-four-inch General as he made his famous ride on his big black horse from Winchester, Virginia, to rouse his men, who had been routed by the rebels at Cedar Creek, and bring them back to the ranks. Soon Gutzon had made a small model of his proposed statue which won the immediate approval of Sheridan's widow and son. But now there was nothing more Gutzon could do on the statue until the model was approved and accepted by the committee, and the committee wasn't scheduled to meet for several weeks.

Meantime Gutzon was free to work on another "pipe-dream." It was strictly a "fun" project. For years Gutzon had studied and admired Abraham Lincoln. He was fascinated by the various moods of Lincoln and he wanted to see if he could combine these moods into a true portrait.

Usually when Gutzon was going to make a statue, he first perfected a clay model. Then a plaster cast of the clay model was made and then the final marble statue was made by copying the plaster figure with the aid of measuring devices. Since Lincoln was to be done purely for his own enjoyment, Gutzon decided he would skip the preliminary steps and start with the marble. Marble was expensive but Gutzon knew a dealer who sold chunks of it that had been piled into the hold of Greek ships for ballast. It was sold for very little when the ships reached America to make room for cargo on the return trip. For a small sum, Gutzon was able to get a three-foot square block of Greek Pantellio marble that was almost dead white.

Mary Montgomery, who was now doing all of Gutzon's

secretarial work, confided to a friend that Gutzon "treated the chunk of marble much the same as a child treats a new toy." The longer he chiseled, the more excited he got. Before long he was carving sixteen hours a day. His hands and fingers were bruised and swollen. He cut and recut the forehead a dozen times and he worked on the mouth for days to capture just the right amount of sadness combined with Lincoln's' roguish sense of humor. Gutzon was trying to picture Lincoln as he had been at the beginning of his first term as president. For six weeks Gutzon chiseled feverishly. He worked straight through the Christmas holidays. When he wasn't actually working on the marble, he was studying the famous life mask of Lincoln done by Leonard Volk, or he was poring over the many photographs he had collected.

One snowy evening shortly after the New Year, Miss Montgomery received a telephone call from Gutzon. "Come quickly and see," he said. "My Lincoln has come to life at last!"

He put the head on display in the window of the foundry where he had most of his statues cast. Lincoln's son, Robert Todd, saw it there and was prompted to write Gutzon, "I have seen your work at the Gorham Company's building, and was deeply impressed by it. I think it is the most extraordinarily good portrait of my father I have ever seen, and it impressed me deeply as a work of art which speaks for itself in the most wonderful manner." He continued, "With your permission I will do myself the pleasure of calling and making your personal acquaintance, as I should like to congratulate you in person on this great success in which I naturally have a peculiar interest."

Others, too, were quick to praise the head. Truman H.

Borglum with his colossal head of Lincoln

Bartlett, a fellow sculptor and Lincoln authority wrote, "I doubt much if any piece of American portrait sculpture made under the most favorable conditions from life, is near the equal of Borglum's head of Lincoln." When William Allen White, the famous editor of the Emporia (Kansas) Gazette saw the head he wrote to Gutzon, "I am enclosing my check for five bones. I wish you would send me three copies of your Lincoln photographed with your name written on them." Then he went on, "I think that Lincoln is one of the most marvelous pieces of sculpture ever done in America."

President Theodore Roosevelt saw the head and asked that it be placed in the White House during the week of February 12th. He wrote Gutzon, "That head of Lincoln grows upon me more and more. I think it one of the finest things I've seen. I especially like it when seen from the right front."

After it came back from Washington, the head was exhibited at the National Sculpture Society show in Baltimore. Before the show had ended, Eugene Meyer, a wealthy New Yorker, purchased the head for eight thousand dollars and presented it to the nation's Capitol. It was formally accepted by the Joint Committee of Congress on the Library on May 8, 1908 and was placed in the rotunda of the Capitol. What had began as a "pipe-dream" became the first and one of the most admired of the many Borglum statues in Washington, D.C.

That same month, Gutzon had another reason to rejoice. Lisa finally agreed to give him a divorce. Two years before, Gutzon had written his legal adviser in California, "I am tired, tired and old. Ever since I was married at twenty-two I have tried to live an older age and forgone my youth." Now Gutzon was forty-one, but when he got word of the divorce he said, "At last I can be young. I have my whole life ahead of me."

During the time the Lincoln head was at the White House the Sheridan committee met and approved Gutzon's model and he began serious work on the large clay model. Instead of making a small model and having it mechanically enlarged as many sculptors did, Gutzon preferred to make his model the same heroic size as the finished bronze.

As the horse and rider began to grow and grow in the studio, Sam Banks complained that he spent more time keeping the mountain of clay on the statue wet than he did taking care of the live horses. Everyday Sam led Halool or Smoke into the studio. They wandered around like two friendly dogs for Gutzon to watch as he worked. One day Julia Percy, a model who had posed for many of Gutzon's female statues, dropped in to watch Gutzon work. Gutzon handed her a lump of sugar. "Here," he said, "let Smoke lick just a little sugar at a time so he will hold his head still. I want to model his neck." Smoke kept licking just like a kitten until he decided Miss Percy wasn't giving enough sugar at a time and he nipped her finger. She shrieked! Smoke jumped! Gutzon's gray eyes flashed and his bushy mustache quivered. Then he saw that Miss Percy was in pain and he rushed over to her with a bucket of cold water, to put her sore thumb in. It wasn't the best treatment for the thumb, but it did restore calm to the studio and made Gutzon forget to be angry about the interruption.

When Gutzon was ready to put the final touches on Sheridan, the army gave Lieutenant Sheridan leave to spend a week at the New York studio to pose for the statue. When the finished statue was cast, two hundred people came to the foundry to watch the pouring of the bronze. It was cast in

Statue of General Sheridan in Washington, D. C.

two pieces—the horse and the rider. Six thousand pounds of metal were used for the horse. This was the first time an American foundry had cast a figure of this great size all in one piece.

The finished statue was placed on a low pedestal in a circle on Massachusetts Avenue in Washington, D. C. It was so located that Mrs. Sheridan could look down on it from a window of her home. President Roosevelt, members of the cabinet, the diplomatic corps, Justices of the Supreme Court—in fact the entire official family of Washington—plus thousands of soldiers and sailors attended the unveiling ceremony. After the statue was unveiled by Mrs. Sheridan, the President introduced Gutzon as "the one whom the distinguished assemblage should wish to see more than any one else present."

These were truly happy times. Gutzon now had two statues in Washington. He was often a guest at the White

House. Somehow, too, he found time to continue civic activities and to pursue his interest in airplanes. He followed closely the experiments of the Wright Brothers and when he learned Orville Wright was going to make a series of test flights for the army at Fort Myer in Washington, D. C., he laid aside his modeling tools and hurried down to the capital.

It was about four o'clock in the afternoon of September 10, 1908 when Gutzon got off the streetcar at Arlington Cemetery. He was so excited by that time that he fairly ran the entire length of the dusty parade ground to a small barn-like shed where, as he put it, "the new bird was roosting." There were about a thousand people milling around, all trying to get a look at the queer, spiderlike contraption. It had two cotton-covered horizontal frames, one above the other, about six feet apart and a motor engine that rested on the bottom plane. The two propellors looked something like fence boards stained green. Despite the fact that the day before Orville Wright had kept his machine in the air for a record sixty-two minutes and fifteen seconds, most of the spectators were skeptical that anything that was heavier than a horse could even get off the ground.

When Wright arrived, a group of troopers helped drag the plane out of the shed and across the field to a little tripod from which hung a weight and from which, along the ground, extended a small rail. The plane was anchored on this rail and the suspended weight was raised. Its falling at the time of the takeoff aided the plane to get immediate speed.

At last the important moment arrived. The motor started and the plane jumped forward. Wright pulled his cap down over his head, waved, and away he slid. He barely cleared the weed tops and then all of a sudden he seemed to mount higher. When he got to the end of the field he turned and

The Wright Brothers airplane that flew at Ft. Myer

came back. Round and round he went. On the forty-second time around, a strong gust of wind caught the plane and it plunged sharply downward. The crowd gasped in alarm, but still he would not come down. It was obvious he was out to break his record of the day before. When he had been up fifty-eight minutes, his assistant climbed on the shed and with chalk marked the minutes on the roof in big letters for Wright to see. On the fifty-third round Wright reached a height of two hundred feet. As he made the fifty-eighth round he had broken his record of the day before and he began his bumpy descent. He had been up sixty-five minutes and fifty-two seconds. As he settled down on the ground, some of the crowd cheered and ran toward the plane. Others just stood speechless. One feeble old man standing near Gutzon took hold of his wife's arm. "Come on," he said as he pulled her toward a waiting horse and buggy, "I don't mind if I go now. I've lived long enough to see everything."

That night Gutzon wrote a friend, "This is no experiment. Man has put, safely and forever, his shod heel into the blue heavens. Wright has added power, a rudder of a piece of cardboard and will rub out the boundaries of the world. Wright's achievement will make our great country even greater."

Next day Mary Montgomery was waiting for Gutzon at the studio to hear all about the wonderful flight. Gutzon came booming in, full of the excitement of the day before. But when he saw Miss Montgomery waiting for him, he forgot all about Orville Wright. He suddenly realized that it was because of her that he had hurried back. "What would I ever do, Peggy," he said with a rather surprised look on his rugged face, "if I came back and you weren't waiting for me." Miss Montgomery had known long ago how much she meant to Gutzon. When he added, "I'd feel a lot safer if you'd marry me," she answered, "I thought you were never going to ask me!"

Borgland

7

On May 19, 1909, Mary Montgomery wrote in her diary, "Here begins the new life. This is the day Dane and I will be married." The ceremony took place in the cottage of Mary's brother, Rev. Marshall Montgomery, at Short Beach, Connecticut. Late in the afternoon the newlyweds boarded a train bound for Lake Algonquin in Canada. For two weeks they camped in the woods amidst evergreens and snowdrifts and made elaborate plans for the "new life."

They returned in time to attend the commencement exercises at Princeton University when Gutzon received an Honorary Degree of Master of Arts from the president of the college, Woodrow Wilson.

Gutzon still wasn't ready to settle down. The Canadian trip was the first he had ever taken that was purely vacation, and he was amazed at how much fun it was. "Let's go to Colorado and fish and see Pike's Peak and Grand Canyon," said Gutzon on their return from Princeton. Mary set the pattern for the years ahead when she answered, "I'm ready to go wherever you go, Dane."

However, Mary would not deny that she was glad when Gutzon finally got his fill of camping and fishing and decided it was time to get back to the Thirty-eighth Street studio.

They had been back in New York only a short time when they were awakened one morning at three by the jingling of the telephone. Before Gutzon took up the receiver, he said, "Papa is dead. I know. I have been thinking about him all day." It was true. He was dead. Several days before, Doctor Borglum had been thrown from a horse. Thinking his injuries only minor, he continued to call on his patients, despite a "nagging pain in his head and back." Then all of a sudden he began to feel worse. When he finally lay down to rest, he never woke up.

Gutzon was glad that he and Mary had stopped off in Omaha for a few days on their way West. He had found his father in such good spirits then. It also made him happy to remember that a year ago, when his father expressed a desire to visit Denmark, Gutzon had borrowed the money so he could have the trip. In fact for years Gutzon had been borrowing to send money to various members of his family. After his father's death he continued to send money to his stepmother until she died in 1911. He frequently loaned money to needy young artists, too. He never bothered to keep track of such loans and was always surprised and even a little hurt when he found that those who loaned money to him did keep records.

At this time, Gutzon was receiving many commissions involving large sums of money, but usually before he was finished he had spent more on the project than he had been paid.

In fact, Gutzon worked just as hard on a statue for which he was to receive practically no pay as he did on a twenty-five or fifty-thousand-dollar project. He spent days and days on a head of Shakespeare for the New Theater in New York

City. Gutzon remarked that he was repaid many times over for his work, when one of the actors remarked on the evening the head was unveiled, that it was the first statue he had seen that portrayed Shakespeare "as the poet and author, instead of as a brewer and landlord."

The Lincoln and Sheridan statues in Washington were beginning to pay dividends now too. As a result of Gutzon's fine work on these statues, he was one of nine sculptors chosen to work on the magnificent new Pan American Union building in Washington. Gutzon was pleased when he found his brother Solon was also among the nine, although a little doubtful, too, because this was the first time he had worked with others. "If it means I am to be a mere tool to trace someone else's ideas, I will turn it down," he said.

Gutzon's fears were unfounded. His statue was to represent North America. It was to stand at the main entrance opposite the statue for South America, which was to be done by Isidore Konti. Nevertheless, neither sculptor imposed his ideas on the other. Both statues show a draped female figure with one arm embracing a young boy. Gutzon's woman is a strong, vigorous character and the boy is full of energy. Konti's figures are more relaxed, suggesting more of a life of ease. On panels above, the two sculptors designed bas reliefs depicting an important moment in history. Gutzon showed Washington bidding farewell to his generals at the close of the Revolutionary War. Konti depicted the meeting of San Martin and Bolivar at Guayaquil.

Gutzon was proud to be associated with such a patriotic work and he was doubly pleased when, at the impressive formal dedication ceremonies, Albert Kelsey, one of the architects of the building, singled out Borglum and Konti for special praise.

Gutzon had another and more important reason to be proud and happy at this particular time. Mary was expecting a baby. Gutzon's delight over the expected child was so intense, it was almost frightening. He wanted a boy but to prove he didn't really care, he referred to the expected heir as "Peggydane." He would have liked to tell everyone he knew, but Mary, who was reserved and shy, insisted that only their closest friends be told.

Gutzon began immediately to look for a place in the country to live. Late in February 1910 he found it—on a piece of beautiful, wooded land on the banks of the Rippowan River on the outskirts of Stamford, Connecticut. There were six or seven little old houses on the land and one larger one that Gutzon thought could be remodeled to make a home. Mary knew when he took her to see the place that he had already made up his mind to buy it. He borrowed the money for the down payment from Eugene Meyer, who had presented the Lincoln head to the Capitol. "We'll start first by remodeling the house," said Gutzon.

Gutzon never really had enough hours to complete his commissions; yet he kept reaching out for more activities. He had just been awarded a contract for a Lincoln statue for the city of Newark, New Jersey. He had gotten the contract through Ralph Lum, one of the executors of the estate of Amos Van Horn who had left a hundred and fifty thousand dollars to be used for three public monuments for Newark—one of Washington, one of Lincoln, and a third a monument to soldiers and sailors. Lum had seen Gutzon's Lincoln in Washington. Gutzon knew that another artist had been given the commission for Newark's Washington statue, but the soldiers and sailors contract was still open and if he could please with his Lincoln he should be able to get the other as well.

At this same time Gutzon was trying to get a contract to do a Lincoln statue for Cincinnati. He made several trips to Ohio to see committee members and they, in turn, visited his New York studio. Countless friends wrote the committee in Gutzon's behalf. Elihu Root, who had served as President Roosevelt's Secretary of State and who was now a United States Senator from New York, wrote that he was so immensely impressed by Gutzon's Lincoln that "when the arrangements were being made for statuary for the new Pan American Building, I insisted that Mr. Borglum should have a part in the work." Robert Todd Lincoln wrote, "It is my belief that Mr. Borglum would make a finer work in every way than anyone I know of. For myself I should not hesitate to give him the commission." Rodin sent a telegram from Paris, "I recommend Gutzon Borglum as a great artist." Small wonder that Gutzon felt quite sure of the award.

Then on March 6, 1910, Gutzon received the greatest disappointment of his life. "Peggydane," a perfect little boy, arrived too soon and did not live. Mary dared not show her own grief. Instead she began to make plans immediately for another "Peggydane," and was successful enough in her effort to make Gutzon look ahead, that on March 25th, his forty-third birthday, he resolved to "build a home at Stamford to be ready for Peggydane whenever we are blessed."

Gutzon immediately hired carpenters and workmen to start remodeling the big house. Despite the lack of a stove and of water, the Borglums moved into the house that was being remodeled. They moved from room to room as the work was being done. On their first wedding anniversary, they celebrated by selecting the site for Gutzon's studio. They had a picnic on the spot and decided that day to call their estate "Borgland." It was late afternoon when they walked

The Borglums' house at Borgland

through the woods up the hill to the house. "This has been as near a perfect day as I've ever had," said Gutzon as they approached the house.

A few moments later the happiness of the day was forgotten when Gutzon received a telegram from one of his friends on the committee for the Cincinnati Lincoln. The commission was to be awarded to George Grey Barnard. Gutzon never was any good at hiding his feelings. He was greatly disappointed, but then he became angry. The Cincinnati contract was definitely lost, Gutzon finally admitted. "But there is one thing I can do," he said, "I can put my whole heart and soul into creating a Lincoln for Newark that will make even Cincinnati sit up and take notice."

Gutzon began by rereading all the material about Lincoln he had accumulated over many years. He made a number of rough sketches for a statue but none suited him. He had difficulty in deciding upon the moment in Lincoln's life that he wanted to portray. He wanted his statue to be more than a mere portrait. He wanted it to tell a story.

Gutzon was on his way home from a trip to Washington when the idea for the Newark Lincoln finally came to him. He had visited the White House and had noticed a bench in the garden. Now, as he was on the train heading back toward New York, he remembered reading that during the most anxious days of the Civil War Lincoln waited until long past midnight for news from the battlefronts. Oftentimes when he received a particularly disturbing message before retiring he would sit on a bench in the White House garden to collect his thoughts.

Gutzon got out his sketchbook and made a small, rough, hasty pencil sketch. Next day, in the New York studio, he quickly made a tiny model of Lincoln sitting on a park bench. Major Richard Tyler, a veteran of the Civil War, saw the model. "When your statue is finished," he asked Borglum, "will I be able to sit on that bench beside Mr. Lincoln?"

"Yes indeed," answered Borglum. "It is my hope to place the statue on the steps in front of the Court House where anyone who feels inclined can sit down beside the great man."

Lum and the other members of the Newark committee had nothing but praise for the little model, so Gutzon proceeded to make a model one and a half times life size. The huge statue was cast in bronze in one piece so that there would be no seams that might crack and mar the surface.

The statue was unveiled on Decoration Day, 1911. On that day, Gutzon and Mary met Theodore Roosevelt, who was to be the principal speaker, at the New York office of *The Outlook*, a magazine of which "Teddy" was the editor, and they went with him in an open car to Newark. It was a gala occasion. Crowds gathered along the streets in Newark to greet the ex-President. When Roosevelt saw the statue he exclaimed, "This doesn't look like a monument at all. It looks real!" Immediately following the unveiling of the statue dozens of children began to gather around it. First one and then another timidly sat down on the bench beside Lincoln. Soon a little girl climbed on Lincoln's knee and another put her arms about his neck. A bootblack stopped and gave Lincoln's shoes a vigorous brushing.

City officials promptly suggested that they put a fence around Lincoln to protect him. Gutzon, whose eyes were misty, shook his head, "I am proud to have created a Lincoln to be loved by little children." No fence was ever built around the statue and today, at almost any time of day, a child may be seen nestled in Lincoln's arm or an adult sitting quietly beside Lincoln on the court house steps in Newark, New Jersey.

For days following the unveiling, words of praise came pouring in to Gutzon. "Your Lincoln is lacking only in the

Borglum's statue of Lincoln on a park bench

heartbeat and the breath of life," wrote Ross Appleton, President of the Security Bank of New York. Felix Frankfurter, an old friend of Gutzon, who was then serving in the Bureau of Insular Affairs in Washington, wrote, "Your Newark statue took permanent hold of me as the most living, intimately knowable Lincoln I have seen."

A few months later when the architect's plans for the Lincoln Memorial in the nation's capital were made public, Gutzon joined a host of other Americans who were critical of putting the rugged Lincoln in a "Greek temple." He wrote Frankfurter, "I read with pain akin to madness of the folly of the plans maturing for the great Lincoln Memorial. A modernized twentieth-century interpretation of a Greek temple to stand there forever on the flats—upon the lawn of Washington, to . . . remind us of that simple great first gift of the West. How . . . do men arrive at these things? Is it possible that Lincoln is to be dehumanized and rolled into the conventional architectural formula so soon! Is it possible the people are so blind that such a thing will be permitted?" Nor did Gutzon confine his criticism to letters. He gave speeches and wrote newspaper articles. The building of the Lincoln Memorial proceeded exactly as was originally planned, and fellow sculptors looked upon Gutzon as a traitor to his profession. "It was my public duty," he stated, "to speak out on a matter that concerned a public monument destined to stand for all time."

Gutzon might have gone on with his criticism of the monument but at the moment he was occupied with affairs at Stamford. Some friends had presented the Borglums with a little cart and a donkey which they named Shamrock. Another friend had given them a black poodle. Gutzon, who never missed a circus when it came to town, named the dog Marcelline, after a famous French clown. Gutzon loved to ride around his estate in the little cart with Marcelline at his side directing and checking the work on the many building projects that were in progress. Old barns were being torn down or moved, a stable for Halool and Smoke was almost finished, and a brook was being dammed to make a pond. The "big" house was practically completed but Gutzon's studio, which was being built of rough granite quarried on the grounds, was only about half finished. Gutzon had rigged up a temporary studio out of a chicken coop and some glass cold-bed frames. Even though he still did most of his work in the New York studio, he liked having a place to work at Stamford since very often building projects demanded that he stay home for a day.

He already had projects in the process of completion in the chicken coop studio. He was putting the final touches on a memorial for North Carolina to Henry Lawson Wyatt, the first Confederate soldier to be killed. He also was working on designs for some medals for the Red Cross. The designs were

Borglum in front of his "chicken coop" studio

being presented to the Red Cross by the American Numismatic Society, of which Gutzon was a member. He took particular pride in the First Aid Medal. On one side was a Red Cross knight kneeling to help a wounded man and on the other side were two women assisting an injured man. This medal was widely used by the Red Cross in first aid contests.

Gutzon thoroughly enjoyed doing medals. A little later he designed, without charge, a medal for School Boy Athletes to be awarded by the New York *Evening Mail*. The managing editor of the *Mail* wrote to Borglum, "The medal itself is a beautiful thing. It expresses most admirably the central thought which is that of development through athletics of a strong and beautiful body rather than competitive speed or skill."

Gutzon still had his eye on the soldiers and sailors monument that was part of the Van Horn bequest to Newark. The committee wasn't ready to act yet, but after the success Gutzon had achieved with the seated Lincoln he was sure he would be approached. This was to be a hundred-thousand-dollar project. "With that much money at my disposal, Peggy," he said, "I can create a monument that will truly do honor to the brave men who have served America in times of war." There were already four or five sketch models for this monument in the chicken coop studio.

When Gutzon went to New York to work, Mary usually went with him. Even though Gutzon had a full-time secretary and several studio assistants, Mary was able to relieve him of many of the routine business affairs which he not only disliked to handle himself but which actually annoyed him. Besides it gave Mary great pleasure to watch Gutzon at work. Gutzon, too, was reluctant to be away from Mary even for a day. She was expecting a baby and after their first sad experience Gutzon was overly anxious for Mary's health. He showered her with tenderness. She watched him mold his deep feelings of reverent admiration for all women into a marble statue called "Atlas." His "Atlas" was a woman bearing the burden of the earth in her arms. "I have always felt that the ancients were wrong," said Gutzon. "It is the woman who must sustain the great responsibilities of life. The sphere which my figure bears is motherhood. She is portrayed in holding the globe, for so the real burdens of life are borne in the arms."

In the New York studio Gutzon also was completing a monument to be placed in Rock Creek Cemetery in Washington, D.C. at the Ffoulke family plot. The Ffoulke's had originally commissioned Daniel Chester French to make the monument but apparently he was unable to please them and they finally awarded the work to Gutzon. He worked on the statue several years before he finally was able to satisfy the family. His completed monument, which he called "Rabboni," was designed as a symbol of faith and hope. It represents Mary Magdalene when she turned from the empty tomb to find Jesus speaking to her. Gutzon himself was quite pleased with the finished statue but he frankly admitted there had been times when he might have given up the project were it not for the fact that he was being paid for his work with several very beautiful tapestries that he really wanted for Stamford.

By the end of the year 1911 the Borglums were pretty much settled in the big, roomy Stamford house. In place of a series of what Gutzon termed "nothing but cubby holes" there were now rooms "where a man could catch his breath." Every weekend the house overflowed with friends from New York. Gutzon's big new studio was well enough along so that he could begin to work in it and gradually he moved more and more of his work from the Thirty-eighth Street studio to Borgland.

Mary, Gutzon, and Marcelline spent a quiet, beautiful New Year's Eve in the new studio. Gutzon built a big fire in the fireplace and then he read aloud to Mary Robert Browning's provocative monologue based on the life of the Italian painter, Andrea del Sarto. At the stroke of midnight, Marcelline joined Gutzon in lustily greeting the New Year and Gutzon danced around the room with him. When the dying fire flickered out, Gutzon carried Mary through the snow to the big house and after depositing her gently on the porch, he rolled in the snow down the hill with Marcelline.

Mary watched from the porch. She knew that much of Gutzon's exuberance was due to his anticipation of Peggydane's arrival. She and Gutzon had voiced no wishes for the coming year, but each knew what wish was in the heart of the other.

Interior of Gutzon's second studio at Borgland

"The Making of a Story"

8

PEGGYDANE WAS a boy! He let out his first lusty cry on the beautiful spring morning of April 9, 1912 and from that moment became Gutzon's most cherished possession. Gutzon named him James Lincoln after his father and his favorite American. He showered on his baby boy the stored-up love from all the years of his longing for a child. A string of nurses came and went because none of them gave baby Lincoln the exacting care Gutzon thought he needed.

At this time, Gutzon was working on a fountain for Bridgeport, Connecticut. It is not surprising that several baby faces were included in its design. There was a drinking fountain for people in the center of a triangular island at an intersection of two wide streets and this was surrounded by three smaller low fountains for horses and dogs. The central figure in the people's fountain was a mermaid with upraised arm carrying a torch to provide light for the fountain; the other arm clasped a baby mermaid. Around the big bowl of the fountain were four infant heads, spouting water from their mouths. The four heads represented the four grandchildren of Nathaniel Wheeler whose heirs had provided the money for the fountain. But all the baby faces in the fountain looked like the infant Lincoln.

Gutzon with Marcelline and his son Lincoln

"He's not only the youngest model I ever used," boasted Gutzon, "but he's the handsomest."

Gutzon had a series of leather-bound books made, with titles lettered in gold on the covers: *Birds of Borgland, Flowers of Borgland, Animals of Borgland, Trees of Borgland.* On fine spring days when the family rode around the estate in the little cart pulled by Shamrock, Mary and Gutzon filled the blank pages of these books with sketches.

Although Gutzon was a newcomer to the Stamford community, he had no intention of being an outsider. "It is my

duty as a citizen to take an active part in the civic and political affairs of my home town," said Gutzon. "Many of my
friends regret that I am not eternally astride a ton of clay,
constantly modeling. They do not realize," he went on, "that
the insistent application of a man's mind or his body to one
subject creates lopsidedness."

His first project was to get lighting for the country road
that ran from town past his place. Then he set about securing
funds to improve some of the more widely traveled roads
around Stamford. He organized a bus company, using bodies
for the buses that he designed himself, for farm folk to use
getting back and forth from town.

When Theodore Roosevelt decided to run for President on
a Progressive ticket, against Woodrow Wilson, a Democrat,
and the incumbent Republican President William H. Taft,
Gutzon went all out to win support in Connecticut for his
friend. At the start of the campaign Roosevelt made the remark, "I feel as fit as a Bull Moose," and so the Progressive
party became known as the Bull Moose party. Gutzon was
about the most active Bull Moose in the nation. He gave
speeches in the Town Hall and when a hall wasn't available
he stood on the corner and never failed to draw a crowd as
he boomed forth against boss-ridden political machines. As a
grand finale to his campaign for Roosevelt, Gutzon organized
a dramatic torchlight parade in which Shamrock was the leading character, wearing an elephant head and trunk over his
rear, as the symbol of the Progressive party.

Roosevelt lost the election but he thought highly enough
of Gutzon's efforts to write him, "In this great fight for ele-
mentary justice and decency, for fair play in the industrial no
less than in the political world, and for honesty everywhere,
there are many men to whom I feel peculiarly grateful, not

only personally but because of what they have done for the people as a whole. You come high among these men; and in this very inadequate but far from perfunctory manner, I wish to express my profound acknowledgment."

Gutzon continued to take an active part in the political affairs of Connecticut. By the time of the state election of 1914 he was asked to allow his name to go on the ballot as Progressive candidate for Lieutenant Governor. He declined, saying, "I could not accept the honor. I am not a statesman. I am a sculptor in the prime of my productive abilities, but I am doing my level best to take interest in public affairs that all good citizens should take."

Despite Gutzon's many civic activities, he spent most of his time "astride a ton of clay." He wasn't happy unless he had three or four statues in the making in his studio at one time and several more in the offing. Each new project was approached with enthusiasm. "I wouldn't waste my time on something that I didn't believe in wholeheartedly," said Gutzon.

While he was campaigning for the Bull Moose party, Borglum was also studying the life of Henry Ward Beecher. He had a commission to make a statue for Plymouth Church in Brooklyn where Beecher had served as pastor for forty years. From the many dramatic incidents in the life of the fiery preacher Gutzon chose to picture him at the time he spoke at a great meeting to raise money to free two slave girls known as the Edmonson sisters. In the completed statue, Beecher is portrayed with the two sisters at his feet.

While the clay Beecher was shrouded with wet cloths awaiting the approval of various committee members, another great orator was coming to life in the Stamford workshop. He was a Midwesterner named John P. Altgeld who had had a stormy career as Governor of Illinois. This statue presented a real challenge to Gutzon's creative and imaginative powers. Twice he had refused to participate in a competition for the Altgeld memorial. The committee had eventually rejected all models submitted in the two competitions on the grounds that they did not fully symbolize the work and character of the former governor, and had asked Gutzon to do the statue. "I never in my life made a statue that was merely a picture of a man. My work always tells a story," Gutzon assured the committee.

Altgeld had fought for shorter working hours and Gutzon portrayed him standing, with a laborer and his wife and child beneath his outstretched hands. The Altgeld Committee thought it was a fine statue but the Chicago Municipal Commission and the State Art Commission thought differently and tried desperately to block the unveiling of the statue in Chicago's Lincoln Park. They maintained that Gutzon had depicted Labor in a servile attitude. Gutzon was not the least perturbed by all the criticism. He attributed it to the fact that the art commissions, "as every other art commission I know of in America, are improperly constituted and incompetent." The statue was unveiled as scheduled on Labor Day and the ceremony was attended by delegations of most of the labor organizations. "Criticism of the design of the statue was wiped away," said a labor spokesman, "by the attendance at the unveiling."

Gutzon's many commissions and speaking engagements demanded that he travel about the country a great deal. Whenever possible, Mary and young Lincoln accompanied him. Gutzon could hardly bear to have Lincoln out of his sight. In the Stamford studio the child was always at his father's side. Since Gutzon was now doing much of his work

Mary Borglum with baby Lincoln

at Stamford, a number of studio helpers and a stenographer lived on the estate. Lincoln remained unaffected by all the attention that was showered on him by these adults. He was a sweet, gentle child and he idolized his father. He had an uncanny perception of his father's changing moods and never knowingly did anything that would displease or distress him. Gutzon talked to his young son much as he would talk to an adult. Lincoln didn't understand some of the conversation but he liked to hear his father talk anyway.

In fact almost everyone enjoyed hearing Gutzon talk,

whether they agreed with him or not. Mary said she never heard Gutzon say a commonplace thing. Gutzon especially enjoyed talking about Abraham Lincoln and was in constant demand as a speaker at Lincoln affairs. He received wide acclaim for his Lincoln Day address at Springfield, Illinois in 1915 and later, when Lincoln's tomb at Oak Ridge Cemetery in Springfield was remodeled, a replica of Gutzon's head of Lincoln was placed at the entrance.

By now, Gutzon's reputation as a sculptor was well established. Satisfied customers came back a second time. Gutzon had done Henry Lawson Wyatt for North Carolina. Now he was asked to do North Carolina's beloved Zebulon Baird Vance, former Governor and United States Senator. The statue was to be placed in Statuary Hall in the Capitol. When the old Hall of the House of Representatives was set apart for use as a National Statuary Hall in 1864, it was decided that each state could place statues of two of its citizens in the Hall. Vance was to be the first North Carolinian to be put there and Borglum was more than proud to execute the work.

About this time he received another request from the South—a request so amazing that even Gutzon, with all his vivid imagination and vision, was somewhat astounded. The request came in a letter from Atlanta, Georgia, written by Mrs. C. Helen Plane, national president of the United Daughters of the Confederacy. First she mentioned that she had seen and admired Gutzon's head of Lincoln in the Capitol. She also mentioned that Gutzon had been highly recommended to her by a young lady named Margaret Etheridge who had years before been helped by Gutzon on a bit of sculpture she was attempting. She closed her letter by asking Gutzon if he would be interested in carving the head of Lee on the side of a mountain in Georgia.

Gutzon was dubious, but the very thought of carving on a mountain excited him. In his many years of studying Lincoln and the Civil War, he had read much about Robert E. Lee.

"It would be a great work, Peggy," said Gutzon. "That is it *could* be a great work, or it could be a great failure." The more Gutzon thought about carving Lee on a mountain, the more enthusiastic he became. He wrote Mrs. Plane that he would come to Georgia to see the mountain and talk over the project. He closed his letter with, "I think you have an opportunity to do something unique in the world."

On August 17, 1915, Gutzon stepped off the train in Atlanta and was greeted by an energetic, determined looking old lady. "I'm Helen Plane," she said crisply. She quickly introduced Gutzon to several other ladies who were with her and they started immediately to the mountain. It was a sixteen-mile drive from Atlanta and on the way the eighty-six-year-old Mrs. Plane told Gutzon some of the background of the idea for the proposed memorial. For years various organizations in Atlanta had discussed the possibility of using Stone Mountain in some way as a memorial to the Confederacy. The United Daughters of the Confederacy had decided to take some positive action. Their idea was to carve a twenty-foot head of Lee near the base of the mountain. Two brothers, Samuel and William Venable, had operated vast quarries at the mountain. Later they had leased the mountain to a granite corporation. William died in 1905 and his half-interest in the mountain reverted to his heirs. Samuel Venable, a bachelor, was still alive and, according to Mrs. Plane, was very much interested in the memorial and was perfectly willing to donate a twenty-foot square spot of his mountain for such a worthy cause.

All this sounded quite reasonable to Gutzon. But then he

hadn't seen Stone Mountain. Even when he saw it from a distance, a gigantic, lonely boulder in the middle of an almost
level area, he was not prepared for what faced him when they
got within a few hundred feet of the steep side of the mountain. It was a sheer, bald wall some nine hundred feet high and
a mile and a half wide. "It's easily five times as high as Niagara
Falls," mused Gutzon as he looked in stunned silence.

Little Mrs. Plane was a bit annoyed with Gutzon's seeming
lack of enthusiasm. "Are you interested?" she quipped. For the
first time in his life Gutzon was at a loss for words. "What
you are proposing," he finally blurted out, "would look like a
postage stamp on the side of a barn."

The ladies were crushed. They had counted on this great,
imaginative artist from the North. "Well," said Mrs. Plane,
"we may as well get back to town for the luncheon and reception."

"You go," said Gutzon. "Give me a little time to think. I'll
figure something out." The ladies told him how to get to
Samuel Venable's summer home at the end of the mountain.
"Call us when you've thought of something," said Mrs. Plane.
"We'll be waiting." And they went off and left him.

The looks on the ladies' faces plainly indicated to Gutzon
that they didn't expect him to think of anything, and at that
moment he felt they were right. The longer he gazed at that
big granite mass, the lonelier he felt. His common sense told
him to go back to Borgland and forget about the ladies and
their impossible dream. But Gutzon knew he wouldn't leave
until he at least had a substitute plan to suggest to those
gracious Southern ladies. Already he was beginning to feel
something of the valor and the courage of the men who had
fought for what they believed was right.

But nothing had come to mind by the time he went to

meet Samuel Venable. "Call me Sam," said the cordial Southern gentleman. At noon Gutzon met Sam's mother, who was
called Mother Venable, his two sisters, Leila and Elizabeth,
their husbands, Dr. James N. Ellis and Frank Mason, and the
two Mason children. Sam seemed to think it natural that Gutzon would want to study the mountain for awhile and he invited him to stay at "Mount Rest."

Gutzon himself didn't exactly know when the idea came
to him to carve the whole story of the Confederacy on the
side of the mountain. But after three days of viewing the
mountain by day as well as by moonlight, Gutzon had a plan
to suggest.

He waited until after supper. Then he asked Sam to come
out with him and look at the mountain. "Sam, see if you can
see what I see," said Gutzon. While Venable looked, Gutzon
described a procession of Confederate soldiers coming down
off the top and across the mountain—some walking, some on
horseback, some with guns. In the center were Robert E. Lee,
Stonewall Jackson, and Jefferson Davis. Off to the other side
were hosts of Confederate infantrymen.

"Pretty hard to get all that in a twenty-foot square of mountain," was Sam's comment.

"I know," said Gutzon. "I need the whole side of the mountain. I thought I'd better ask you about it before I tell my
plan to Mrs. Plane and her ladies. What should I tell them,
Sam?"

Sam thought awhile. "I believe you're really serious," he
said. "It's a wonderful, impossible idea, but I'll go along with
it. I'll do whatever I can to help. Tell the good ladies they
can have the whole side of the mountain."

Once the idea had caught fire in Gutzon's mind there was
no stopping him. Mrs. Plane's reaction was, "Where would we

ever get enough money for such a tremendous undertaking?"
"I'll help solicit funds," Gutzon replied. "I'll give speeches in
the North and I know I can get financial help for the project."
Before Gutzon returned to Stamford, he had agreed to attend
the national convention of the United Daughters of the Confederacy in San Francisco in October to explain the project.

By October Gutzon had already spoken about the proposed
memorial to a number of civic organizations in New York as
well as to a group of businessmen assembled at the Metropolitan Club in Washington, D.C. He had also gotten his
brother Solon to give talks to publicize the project. Gutzon
was so full of enthusiasm himself that he had no trouble at
all winning the support of the members of the United Daughters of the Confederacy at San Francisco.

These busy days left Gutzon little time for doing "pipe-
dreams" purely for his own enjoyment. However he did man-
age to do a few projects that were almost as rewarding. One
was a monument to Robert Louis Stevenson. Through his
old friend Bob Davis, Gutzon learned that a committee had
been formed at Saranac Lake, New York, to erect some kind
of memorial to Stevenson who had spent the winter of 1887-
88 at Saranac. "The committee has lots of enthusiasm," Davis
told Gutzon, "but unfortunately they have very little money."
Gutzon wasn't concerned about the money. "It's high time
America paid recognition to men of creative genius," he said.

In September 1915, after his return from Stone Mountain,
Gutzon made a trip to Saranac Lake in the Adirondack Mountains. He got there early in the morning and went directly to
the little cottage where Stevenson had lived. Stevenson, who
suffered from tuberculosis, had come there to be under the
care of Dr. Edward Livingston Trudeau. Old Mr. and Mrs.
Andrew Baker, owners of the cottage, showed Gutzon the

room where Stevenson lay in bed and smoked countless ciga-
rettes and wrote and littered the floor with discarded manu-
scripts. Andrew, a woodsman, told Gutzon that in the evenings
they huddled around a wood stove and listened to Stevenson
spin his yarns. After everyone else had gone to bed Stevenson
would bundle up in his heavy fur coat and cap and walk about
for hours on the verandah.

In the afternoon Gutzon talked with Doctor Trudeau. By
evening, when he met with the committee, he was filled with
enthusiasm for the project and he happily donated his services
so that the memorial could be done at once. Within a month
the memorial plaque was finished.

The dedication date was set for October 30th. Gutzon went
up to Saranac the day before to make sure the plaque was
properly placed on the verandah of the Baker cottage. The
plaque portrayed Stevenson as he had nightly walked on the
porch. The inscription read: "Here dwelt Robert Louis Stevenson during the winter 1887-88." There was a quotation from
Stevenson which read:

"I was walking in the verandah of a small cottage outside the hamlet of Saranac. It was winter, the night was
very dark, the air clear and cold, and sweet with the
purity of forests. For the making of a story here were
fine conditions. 'Come,' said I to my engine, 'let us make
a tale.' "

The day was an ideal one for the unveiling. There were
low-hanging clouds and a chill wind blowing down from the
mountains carrying with it a typical Scotch mist. "Just like
many of the days when Stevenson was here," said Baker. A
crowd of several hundred gathered to watch Mrs. Baker unveil

the plaque. "Yes," she said as she gazed at it, "it's just the way he looked when he was here."

Doctor Trudeau was too ill to attend the unveiling. He died the following month, and soon a group of his grateful patients asked Gutzon to make a statue of their beloved physician. Again Gutzon responded by donating his labor. His completed portrait in marble and bronze shows Trudeau seated out of doors with a rug over his knees. After seeing the statue a friend wrote to Gutzon, "It seems to tell the whole life story of an extraordinary man. And I am told you saw him once! With the genius to do magnificent things like this, to create and to embody the living likeness of a great man, why, why, why do you waste your precious time on anything else?"

"No one seems to understand," said Gutzon, "that it is my deep interest in the affairs of my country and my fellow men that gives me whatever insight I may have to put living spirit into my works."

Gutzon and World War 1

9

ON GUTZON's forty-ninth birthday, March 25, 1916, he received "the most wonderful gift in the world." Mary presented him with a baby daughter. Earlier that month Gutzon had taken Mary and Lincoln to Georgia so his second child could be born near Stone Mountain. They named the little girl Mary Ellis after her mother and Dr. James Ellis who brought her into the world.

The date for the formal dedication of Stone Mountain as the memorial site was set for May 20, 1916. Gutzon was jubilant. At last he had a project big enough to tax all his creative and imaginative powers. Nothing could stop him now!

On the day of the dedication, Gutzon sat on the speakers' platform that had been built on the level ground in front of the mountain. He gazed at the giant Confederate flag hanging against the cliff. He was beginning to feel the impact of the staggering commitment he had made. Then his eyes wandered searchingly over the crowd that had gathered. At last he saw what he was looking for—Mary with Mary Ellis in her arms and Lincoln by her side. "Some day," mused Gutzon, "Lincoln and Mary Ellis will be proud to tell their children about this day."

When it was Gutzon's turn to make his address, he frankly admitted that "the vast precipice we are planning to carve has its terrors and dangers; the mountain is a ruthless elemental fact, cold, stubborn." But he spoke with such confidence that no one had any doubt about his success.

In the absence of Sam Venable, who was ill, Doctor Ellis presented the deed to the part of the mountain designated as the Memorial Reservation to the United Daughters of the Confederacy. A great granite block, a cornerstone that marked the boundary, was set in place. It bore the inscription:

1916 May 20
The face of this granite mountain and adjacent
land was presented by Samuel Hoyt Venable on
behalf of William Hoyt Venable and himself to
men and women of America for the purpose of
perpetually honoring the memory of the Southern Confederacy.

The fanfare and the cheering were over. Mary and Gutzon were leaving when they heard a spectator remark, "I guess that Borglum fellow is a pretty good stone carver, but how is he going to get up there on that rock so he can carve anything?"

"He doesn't know, Peggy," said Gutzon, "that for days I've been wondering the same thing."

"You'll think of something," said Mary confidently.

Gutzon had only two thousand dollars with which to begin the work. After much consideration he decided to use the money to build a stairway down the mountain. This in itself was quite a feat. Fortunately Gutzon had already met Jesse Tucker, a fearless young man he thought could do the job. Tucker did carpentry work for Venable and with his little crew of men had constructed the platform for the dedication ceremonies. But Gutzon wouldn't have noticed Tucker on account of that. It was the casual way he had crossed the red danger line and crept down over the top of the mountain to insert spikes on which to anchor the cable for the thirty-by-fifty foot Confederate flag that had won Gutzon's admiration.

Before the Borglums returned to Stamford, Gutzon arranged with Tucker to begin work constructing a four-hundred-and-eighty foot stairway from the top of the mountain to a point where Gutzon planned to begin work on the central figures. Gutzon promised to return to Georgia after he had conferred with a firm of engineers on some of the mechanical problems.

Mary and the children went directly to Borgland. Gutzon stopped off in Washington to catch up on the political situation. The Republican National Convention was to be held shortly in Chicago and Gutzon was anxious to do whatever he could to help unite the Republican and the Progressive parties. Gutzon's choice for presidential nominee was Major General Leonard Wood. He conferred with ex-President Roosevelt and understood that if Roosevelt himself could not be nominated he would support Wood. It was then that Gutzon decided to attend the convention and act as a sort of intermediary between the two parties in the hope of winning the nomination for General Wood, if Roosevelt were not chosen.

Gutzon was no politician, and the convention turned out to be nothing but a heartbreaking experience for him. He never knew what was actually happening among the old-time politicians, but he did know, as did everyone there, that Roosevelt didn't have a chance, and he tried to get Roosevelt to send a telegram indicating his support of Wood. The Republicans and Progressives finally united with Justice of the Supreme Court Charles Evans Hughes as their candidate. At

the last minute Roosevelt sent a telegram throwing his support to Senator Henry Cabot Lodge of Massachusetts. Gutzon
took Roosevelt's decision not to support Wood as a personal
affront, and left Chicago heartily disgruntled.

On the way to Stamford, Gutzon stopped over in Cleve-
land, Ohio, to confer with Lester Barlow, head of the Brown
Hoist Machinery Company, about constructing working sta-
tions for carvers on Stone Mountain. Barlow was an inventor
and showed tremendous interest in the project. "I'll send you
some ideas in a few weeks," he assured Gutzon.

Toward the end of June Gutzon took Lincoln with him to
Washington to attend the impressive ceremonies for the unveiling of the bronze statue of North Carolina's Governor
Vance in Statuary Hall. Gutzon would have gladly taken
Mary Ellis too, but Mary, who rarely failed to support Gutzon
no matter what he wanted to do, would not allow it. She said
she could understand Gutzon's wanting to take his young son
traveling anywhere, any time, but she didn't think that was
the proper way to raise a girl.

Gutzon was quick to point out that the things Lincoln was
doing were all contributing toward making him a more informed citizen. "Besides," he said, "Lincoln has fun." Lincoln
did have fun. Shortly after the trip to Washington, Gutzon
took him on the ferry boat to visit the Statue of Liberty on
Bedloe's Island. They climbed way up in Miss Liberty's arm
so Gutzon could make a careful survey of the torch in Liberty's
hand.

The New York World was then engaged in a nationwide
campaign to raise funds to provide proper lighting for the
Statue of Liberty and for the remodeling of the torch so that
it would simulate a living flame. H. Herbert Magdsick of the
General Electric Company was in charge of the planning and

execution of the lighting of Liberty and he had called on Gutzon to supervise the artistic remodeling of the torch.

Gutzon carried Lincoln on his shoulders as they climbed the 168 steps to Liberty's torch. They went out on the balcony at the base of the torch and Gutzon pointed toward the land. "Take a good look, Lincoln," he said. "You're looking at the greatest country in the world." Lincoln wasn't sure just what his father was talking about so he said, "I think so too, Daddy."

After conferring with Edgar H. Bostock, a noted glazing expert, Gutzon set to work drawing detailed plans for remodeling the torch. He used six hundred sections of amber cathedral glass mounted in cutaway sheets of bronze. The torch was lighted with a lighthouse lens which produced twenty thousand candle power and, to put a quiver into the flame, fifteen five-hundred candle power gas-filled electric lamps were placed on a series of flashers.

From the day many years ago when Gutzon had waved goodbye to Liberty as he sailed to France, he had admired Bartholdi's statue as a true artistic symbol of America's liberty. It was one of the great moments of his life when President Wilson gave the wireless signal to turn on the newly installed floodlights and Gutzon saw for the first time the full effect of the powerful flickering flame he had created.

Gutzon had often wondered how August Bartholdi felt when he created a statue that would surely stand for all time. "Maybe when I finish Stone Mountain," mused Gutzon, "I'll know."

Gutzon received an enthusiastic letter from Tucker telling him the steps down the mountain were almost finished. "Already," Tucker wrote, "we are having about fifty visitors a day." He closed with, "When will you be down?"

"I'll be down right after the first of the year," answered Gutzon. "Am bringing Lester Barlow, an engineer, with me. Surely the three of us can work out a way to get the workmen onto the face of the mountain."

When Gutzon and Barlow got to Georgia they did work something out. It was a kind of leather harness, with a seat attached, that buckled around a workman's waist. The harness was attached to a steel cable which was securely fastened to a wheel hoist, or winch, at the top of the mountain. A winch operator at the top could easily lower or raise a man in the saddle seat over the face of the mountain. The man in the seat had his arms free for working and he could push himself along with his feet over quite an area.

By means of this simple device Gutzon went all over the surface of the rock. He took measurements and made detailed charts showing bulges and imperfections that might be governing factors in the placing of his design. He also was able to

An early model of the carving for Stone Mountain

indicate to Tucker where he wanted workers' platforms to be anchored to the mountain. When this work was under way Gutzon went back to the Stamford studio to make a working model of the central figures to be carved on the mountain.

On April 6, 1917 America declared war on Germany. Tucker promptly joined the army. Gutzon realized that no one would be interested in spending time or labor on a war memorial, or any other kind of memorial, when America was engaged in a war. Sadly he packed away his sketches and his models. "Stone Mountain will still be there waiting for me when America emerges victorious," said Gutzon. He had, however, made a number of appointments with engineering firms to discuss problems of mountain carving and he decided to go ahead and get the information even though it might be some time before work in Georgia was resumed.

In this connection, he visited a firm in Dayton, Ohio. After he had finished his business, he decided to take a tour through an airplane factory. With America at war, he was extremely interested in her efforts to get planes to the front. Gutzon was much disturbed by what he called "total lack of knowledge of the men in charge, both of the subject and the technique involved in plane construction."

He immediately wrote a letter to Joseph P. Tumulty, secretary to President Wilson, expressing his distress at weaknesses in aircraft production. After an exchange of letters, President Wilson wrote Borglum on January 2, 1918:

> "Knowing the earnest and loyal purpose with which you have written me, I have conferred with the Secretary of War and, at his request and my own hearty concurrence, I urge you to come at once to Washington, lay the whole matter frankly and fully before the Secretary,

and by your own investigation discover the facts in this business. The Secretary of War assures me that he will be delighted to clothe you with full authority to get to the bottom of every situation, and that he will place at your disposal the services of Mr. Stanley King, a member of his own personal staff, if you desire to have his counsel in your inquiries. The Secretary further says that he will bring you into personal contact with General Squier, whom you doubtless already know personally, and will direct that every facility of inquiry be placed at your disposal. When you have thus investigated, if the other experts whom you suggest in your letter of December 25 still seem desirable to be appointed you can say so to the Secretary; and in the event of any difference of judgment between you, which seems to me impossible, I would be most happy to have a report from you personally to me on any phase of the matter which remains in the slightest degree doubtful in your mind."

Gutzon, of course, dropped everything and went immediately to Washington. He was assigned a room on the second floor of the War Department office right across the hall from the office of the Secretary of War. In less than a month he had accumulated enough material, he felt, to indicate that the United States Government wasn't getting a proper return on the millions that was being spent on aircraft production. He was unable to get an appointment to present his report personally to the President. Instead, the President wrote: ". . . Before I see you, may I not take the liberty of making this request, that you put your report in writing for my mature consideration and that you attach to it the material upon which it is based? . . . I must regard our relationship in this matter as entirely confidential and express the hope that you will not commit any of the matter to others, not even to stenographers."

So Gutzon reluctantly turned in his written report and went home. His report contained serious accusations against individuals in the aero department as well as against airplane factories. He expected the President to take some immediate drastic action as a result of his report. When no such action was forthcoming and when, after repeated efforts, he was unable to see the President, Gutzon took his claims of malpractices to the press. Eventually it all led to a Department of Justice investigation of alleged profiteering but not before President Wilson and Borglum had a public feud. On April 15th, President Wilson wrote Borglum:

"I am afraid that you have for some time been under a serious misapprehension. You call my attention to the fact that you were not supplied with suitable expert assistance in the investigation which you, of your own motion, undertook of the aircraft production. You will remember that at the beginning you wrote to me saying that you feared and believed that there were very serious errors not only, but serious bad practices, in the aircraft production, and after consulting with the Secretary of War I wrote you that if that was your impression, you were, of course, at liberty to examine any evidence that was in our possession. I never at any time constituted you an official investigator. I merely gave you the right to look into the matter of your own motion, and I am sure that the letter which the Secretary of War provided you with he gave you with the same purpose and idea. We have wished at every point to assist you and to make possible for you what you wished to do, but we have at no time regarded you as the official representative of the administration in making the investigation. If I had so regarded you, I would, of course, have supplied you with such assistance as you feel you have lacked."

On May 7th the President ordered an official probe of the Borglum charges and on the same day Gutzon wrote an open letter to the press attacking the President for his lack of concern. He ended his letter with, "Why is it that placing the truth before the authorities fails for months to meet with response and finally with brusque rebuke, and why, after the work is done and delivered a month or more, I should receive a letter from you refuting the authority which alone brought me to Washington and under which I had worked so long? . . . I am now certain my services have at least compelled some kind of an investigation and I have at least informed the country of its needs and the camouflage deliberately planned by a group of men entrusted with a great arm of our military machine has come to an end."

Gutzon was hurt, distressed, and puzzled by the whole affair. Afterwards he wondered why Wilson, whom he had opposed in two presidential campaigns, had "urged" him to make the investigation in the first place. "Well," said Mary philosophically, "he knew you were no politician but that you were a patriotic American citizen. Then, when your report disagreed with what his official staff was telling him, he naturally turned against you. At least you have made the nation aware of the situation and that in itself is an accomplishment."

Gutzon continued to fuss publicly and privately over the

airplane situation, but that didn't stop him from doing his part toward helping to maintain a free world. Through a young assistant in his studio, an Austrian named Micka, Gutzon became interested in the efforts of a group of Europeans to form the independent republic of Czechoslovakia. Gutzon got acquainted with their leader, Thomas Masaryk, who was in Washington trying to get funds to help the cause. He learned that a large number of foreigners in America were volunteering to fight in Europe for Czechoslovakia. These volunteers were outfitted and sent abroad by the French Military Mission, but they had no place to assemble while they were awaiting transportation. So Gutzon built a camp for them at Borgland. Hundreds of them came from all over the United States. Mary taught them French and helped take care of them when they were sick. She made them a flag of the new republic. When the boys needed supplies, Gutzon helped them put on a colorful pageant at Borgland to raise funds. He attended meetings with Masaryk on the formula-

Czechoslovakian pageant at Borgland

tion of a constitution for the new state. He listened spell-bound when the great musician Ignace Paderewski pleaded the cause of freedom before a tremendous audience in Carnegie Hall.

Paderewski and Borglum were both creative artists and they were both zealous patriots. Small wonder then that a close and lasting friendship developed between the two.

The Armistice ending the war was signed on November 11, 1918. Gutzon had done virtually no sculpturing during the war years. Consequently he had had no income. He had mortgaged Borgland to make the airplane investigation. While the Czech camp was theoretically supported by donation, when money came in too slowly, Gutzon, in his usual fashion, paid the bills and then forgot about them. "I'll soon have enough commissions to pay all my debts," was his optimistic reply to creditors who made rather pressing demands.

Gutzon's own financial problems didn't keep him and Mary from helping struggling young creative artists. The last of the volunteer soldiers had barely left the Czech barracks when new tenants moved in. Gutzon allowed Michio Ito, a Japanese instructor of dance and mime, who had more talent than money, to use the vacated barracks for a dance studio. Angna Enters, the model for Borglum's torso of a dancer, was one of Ito's pupils.

When Ito moved out, other dancers moved into the barracks. Also, there were always three or four struggling young artists working in the studio with Gutzon. And they were not only welcome in the studio, but they were also welcome at the big round oak table in the dining room at mealtimes.

Gutzon's first statue to be unveiled following the Armistice was one he had taken particular pleasure in doing. It was a memorial to a flyer, James Rogers McConnell, a young University of Virginia student, who was killed early in the war flying for France. Some years before, Gutzon had worked on a figure of a human with wings as a memorial to the Wright Brothers. This was never completed so he incorporated some of his ideas into the McConnell statue. The finished memorial shows a figure of a young man with vast wings attached to his arms. He is standing tiptoe on a globe as if he were just ready to take flight. Young McConnell's father, who attended the unveiling at the University of Virginia, wrote Borglum of the statue, "It is magnificently beautiful, comprehensively expressive, and highly inspiring." A replica of the head of "The Aviator" is in the Corcoran Art Gallery in Washington, D. C.

Before the war Gutzon had acquired a six-ton block of fine Grecian marble. In 1919, when Colonel Samuel P. Colt, chairman of the United States Rubber Company, expressed a desire to have Gutzon do a head of Lincoln for him, Gutzon said, "I have a big chunk of marble just waiting for me to uncover the Lincoln that I know is within it."

It did not take him long to chisel a colossal head of Lincoln. Colt displayed the four-and-a-half-ton finished head in the show window of his company for some time before it was removed to his home. Later the head was acquired by the Detroit Institute of Arts.

The following year, when Gutzon was in serious financial difficulty, Colt loaned him ten thousand dollars. Gutzon insisted that he "lend" Colt three of his most beloved marble "pipe-dreams," including "Atlas," as collateral. Unfortunately Gutzon never was able to redeem the statues.

In the Stamford studio another Sheridan on horseback was coming to life. This one was for Chicago's Lincoln Park.

Borglum and Mary Ellis standing in front of the partially
completed statue of Sheridan in the Stamford studio

Gutzon was also hard at work on models to submit to the
Newark committee for the Van Horn soldiers' and sailors'
monument. It took nine models to satisfy himself and the
committee.

When the pictures and description of the proposed monument for Newark appeared in the paper, many fellow sculptors declared it an impossible task. Gutzon's monumental
work, which was to tell the story of our nation in the Revo-

Gutzon's third studio at Borgland, covered with tarpaulin

lutionary, Civil, and World wars included forty-two people and two horses. It was to measure forty-two feet in length and the average figure was to be seven feet, eight inches tall. Gutzon, who was now thinking in terms of carving a mountain, didn't think it was unusually big. "A puny statue could never tell the heroic story of the American soldier and sailor," he said. He agreed to complete the bronze monument by April, 1923.

Since the Stamford studio was already occupied by the partly finished Sheridan, Gutzon began the clay model of the war monument out-of-doors. He hired workmen to construct a new studio around him as he worked. The studio was a Gothic structure built of rocks dragged from the bed of the river by horses. The armature for the statue was made of tree trunks.

By the middle of the summer the framework was up and the first covering of clay was over it. When the walls of the studio were high enough to protect the monument Gutzon bought huge tarpaulins and Mary sewed them together to make a roof for the studio. The tarpaulin puckered a bit and didn't quite cover the entire top so after a time Gutzon replaced it with an old circus tent.

Gutzon had two fine assistants, Luigi Del Bianco and

Hugo Villa who aided him tremendously in mechanical work, such as laying on the clay. This in itself was no small job since the Newark memorial was to require forty tons of clay before the model was completed.

When Ralph Lum, Gutzon's good friend on the committee, saw the size of the armature, he began to be concerned over the cost of casting such a tremendous thing into bronze. Gutzon was sure he would have plenty of money—after all he was getting a hundred thousand dollars to do the work. To satisfy Lum, he asked for three bids on casting, and then went on working at top speed.

At noontimes Mary and Mary Ellis often came from the house with a picnic basket and the morning mail to persuade Gutzon to pause long enough to eat. Lincoln grumbled constantly because he had to go to school. He thought it was much more fun to stay home and watch his father build statues.

The day the first bid came Mary made a special trip to the studio. Gutzon read it and handed it to her. "Obviously it's a typing error," he said. The bid was for one hundred twenty-three thousand dollars. It wasn't an error. The other two bids were only slightly less. It never occurred to Gutzon to reduce the size of his statue. He simply kept on writing letters until he located a foundry that agreed to cast the statue for twenty thousand dollars. It meant shipping the plaster model to Italy but, "that's no problem," Gutzon assured Lum. "It's to be cast in sections so packing will be reasonably simple."

Though the work on hand was more than enough to occupy his mind, Gutzon never for a moment forgot about Stone Mountain. Captain Tucker had visited Stamford at the close of the war and indicated his desire to continue work with Gutzon when the project was resumed. Later, in the spring

Mary Borglum with Mary Ellis

of 1921, he had made a careful survey of conditions at Stone Mountain and wrote, reporting on needed repairs. He urged Gutzon to come to Georgia "to see for yourself." Gutzon had told Tucker that he would come as quickly as possible.

Now, with Sheridan almost finished and the war memorial well underway, Gutzon decided to make a quick trip to Stone Mountain. He had worked out a plan for scaffolding the area where the center group was to be located and he was anxious to get the work started. When the old steps were repaired, Gutzon wanted several platforms anchored to the side of the mountain to house the needed working equipment. Tucker was ready to go to work whenever he got the signal.

Sam Venable and Forest Adair, another loyal supporter

of the project, had already raised a few thousand dollars—enough to get Tucker started on the steps and scaffolding. It was obvious by now that the United Daughters of the Confederacy could never finance the project alone. A group of interested civic leaders joined with the original organization, and formed the Stone Mountain Confederate Monumental Association, to help with financing. Mrs. Plane became president-emeritus of the executive board and an Atlanta businessman named Hollins Randolph became president.

Gutzon didn't concern himself much with this organization. He was chiefly interested in getting the preliminary work done so he could start carving, though he had not yet figured out a way to get his design onto the mountain. He had already tried going down in the harness and painting it on, but at that close range it was impossible to keep any sense of proportion. It occurred to him that if he could project a photograph of his design onto the mountain, all he would have to do would be to trace the picture. He knew that the most powerful projection machine made had a range of about three hundred feet, and he needed one with a range of eight hundred feet.

"You go ahead with the scaffolding," he told Tucker, "and I'll go back to Borgland and get somebody to build us a projector."

Stone Mountain Tragedy

10

"It can't be done," the photographic equipment experts told Borglum when he asked them to build a projector powerful enough to show his pictures on the side of the mountain.

"Then," said Gutzon, "I'll have to design a projector myself." He discussed his problem with Charles d'Emery, a young photographer from Stamford, who had taken a number of pictures at Borgland of statues in various stages of production. Gutzon admired the fine, artistic work d'Emery turned out, and d'Emery, a perfectionist himself, never minded when he had to take a picture three or four times to achieve just the effect Gutzon desired. Charles d'Emery gave Gutzon much advice and information on the technical aspects of photography. Gutzon then consulted E. S. Porter of the Precision Machine Company of New York City who agreed to do some experimenting with Gutzon's ideas.

Meanwhile Gutzon turned his attention to the avalanche of work awaiting him in the New York studio and in the two studios at Borgland. In New York he completed the bust of King Christian Ninth of Denmark which was to be placed in the Christianborg Castle in Copenhagen. Funds for the statue had come from the contributions of several thousand Danes in twenty-two states. Naturally this was a statue in which Gutzon took particular pride. He was well rewarded for all his efforts when Thorvald Jorgensen, architect of the new castle, after seeing the bust, wrote Gutzon, "I am very surprised that a man who never saw the King can give something so good after pictures only."

Sharing the old studio at Stamford with the military leader, Sheridan, was a bust of William Dempster Hoard, an agricultural leader. Hoard, a former governor of Wisconsin, was one of the founders of modern dairying methods. The memorial was to be one of the first dedicated to agriculture and Gutzon was anxious to do something especially fine. Two models had already been submitted to the committee and now, in November 1921, members of the Hoard family were coming to Stamford to view the third model. They made a few minor suggestions which Gutzon carried out while they watched. The completed statue was placed at the entrance to the College of Agriculture at the University of Wisconsin where, according to the Memorial Committee, it "will be in daily view of thousands of students in the years to come, and will serve as an inspiration to lead them to a far better appreciation of the importance of the dignity of farming."

"If it will do that," said Gutzon, "then it is worth all the time and effort it has cost me."

The Chicago Sheridan and the Newark War Memorial, of course, consumed most of Gutzon's time. After working on Sheridan for months, Gutzon was still not satisfied with his model. Despite the fact that Bianco, Villa, Mary, and everyone else who saw the Sheridan, thought it was good, Gutzon didn't. One day he took an axe and chopped the front legs off the horse. "Now," said Gutzon with satisfaction, "I can fix it. I'd rather be late delivering it, than give Chicago something less than perfect. Fifty years from now no one will care whether I was late or not. But they will care if they don't have a good statue."

On January 31, 1922, Solon Borglum died suddenly as a result of an emergency appendectomy. Gutzon was so grief-stricken that for weeks Sheridan and the War Memorial were all but abandoned. On March 1st Gutzon wrote a beautiful tribute to his brother for the New York *Times* in which he said, "The untimely passing of Solon Borglum is a loss to permanent values in America's cultural development . . . that cannot be replaced."

When Gutzon finally did get down to work, he changed the Sheridan three times before he was satisfied. He had chosen to again portray Sheridan at the time of the Winchester ride. But in this statue the horse reared back, his two front feet off the ground, and his head turned as if at a touch of the bridle.

Gutzon was waiting for the Chicago committee to come and give their final approval to the clay model when he received a call to meet with a committee in Raleigh, North Carolina concerning a memorial to an early governor of the state, Charles Brantley Aycock. Borglum met with the committee on July 5, 1922 and on July 6th he wired Mary, "Returning this afternoon, have contract for eighteen thousand dollars." The money for the statue came entirely from donations of school children and North Carolinians who revered the memory of their beloved governor.

With Stone Mountain always looming in the background, Gutzon drove himself day and night during the fall and winter of 1922-1923 to complete all his commissions so he would be free to devote his full time to the Georgia work. But somehow nothing seemed to go smoothly. The South Carolina Committee came to Stamford three times to look at the Aycock statue and each time Gutzon patiently made changes in his clay model. The last time they came, they decided Governor Aycock should be somewhat more robust than Gutzon had pictured him and the entire committee spent three days in the studio while Gutzon added fifty pounds to Aycock's weight.

There were problems with Sheridan, too. This time it wasn't the fault of the committee. They quickly approved the model. But Gutzon had paid little heed to costs and when he finally got estimates for casting the statue in bronze the bids for casting were more than the entire amount Gutzon was receiving to make the statue. Eventually he sent it to the firm of Gusmano Vignali in Italy, who were also casting the War Memorial, but, of course, this meant delaying the dedication.

The greatest problem of all was the War Memorial. Gutzon's contract for casting with the Vignali firm called for his shipping the forty-two figures in eight groups by the end of 1921. By December of 1922, a year later, he had sent only the first four figures and it was obvious that the statue would not be finished in 1923 as Gutzon had promised. Lum was deeply concerned.

As the winter wore on rain and sleet swept down. The tent top sagged and leaked; the modeling clay froze. Big bonfires were built in the studio and still Borglum and his helpers worked in coonskin coats and fur caps. Gutzon couldn't cover his hands, of course, and they were sore and bleeding.

One of the sailors in the group caused a great deal of

trouble. Again and again Gutzon tore the sailor down and completely rebuilt him.

Slowly, a section at a time, the figures that made up the memorial were shipped to Italy for casting. Gutzon knew his dear friend Ralph Lum was constantly being asked by Newark citizens, "When will the monument be ready?" Even so, Gutzon could not bring himself to send a single figure to Italy until he felt it was perfect. In fact each time he sent a section, he regretted it and wished for it back so he could do just "a little more perfecting." As it was, the last section was not shipped until the summer of 1924.

The work might have been completed before then if the Stone Mountain project had not made tremendous demands on Gutzon's time during the spring of 1923. After many conferences and reams of correspondence, the Precision Equipment Company had developed a giant projector which they sent up to Stamford for Gutzon to try. Gutzon had made some slides from his drawings and a giant screen of white bed sheets that he hung about three hundred feet from the projector. Then came the big moment. Quite a crowd had gathered to witness the test. Tucker had even come from the South. Gutzon was nervously trying to focus a slide when all of a sudden Mary Ellis began to shout, "Look, look at all the horses riding in the woods!" Gutzon's design was being thrown far, far beyond the sheets. Never was there such rejoicing at Borgland!

Of course there were some adjustments to be made, but the main problem had been solved and the thousand-pound projector was shipped to Atlanta. Then Tucker and other fearless workers went down in the harnesses at night and painted the design as it was projected on the side of the mountain.

In a relatively short time the necessary machinery and equipment were installed at the mountain. Lester Barlow, the engineer from Ohio, whom Gutzon had consulted at the time of the inception of the memorial, gave Gutzon a great deal of help. The problem of removing large quantities of unwanted stone was solved by the suggestion of a sightseer at the mountain, a Belgian engineer named Jean Vanophem who outlined to Gutzon a method for using light charges of dynamite.

Actual carving of Lee's head began on June 18, 1923. Villa came down from Stamford to help.

The date for the Lee unveiling was set for January 19, 1924 and for six weeks before the men worked day and night in eight-hour shifts. Gutzon often worked round the clock.

Mary took the children out of school and came to Stone Mountain for a two-week visit so they could all be with Gutzon at the time of the unveiling. "He needs us," she said. Only Bianco remained at Borgland. He was working on the final plaster casts of the Newark memorial.

Eleven-year-old Lincoln followed his father all over the scaffolding. He was with him day and night. It never occurred to Lincoln that carving a mountain was unusual.

The day before the unveiling Gutzon and Mary gave a luncheon for visiting dignitaries on Lee's shoulder. Some of the visitors paled as they climbed gingerly down the wooden steps over the precipice of the mountain to reach the luncheon table. The head of Lee was, of course, covered so as not to be viewed until the actual unveiling. Luncheon of southern fried chicken, hot biscuits, and hot coffee was prepared by Hetty McCurdy who operated a little inn at the base of the mountain, and who was a devoted admirer of the entire Borglum family.

Luncheon on Lee's shoulder at Stone Mountain

January 19, 1924, the one hundred and seventeenth anniversary of the birth of Robert E. Lee, was a misty, gray day. At three in the afternoon the ninety-four-year-old gentlewoman of the Old South, Mrs. Plane, was carried on to the platform in Gutzon Borglum's arms. A few moments later she gave the signal to unveil the twenty-one-foot head of Lee. When the flags that draped the statue parted, spectators gazed in awed silence. The stillness was broken by the thin outcry of an old man in a gray uniform: "It is Lee, it is Lee!"

Gutzon wasn't exactly sure what happened after that, except that there was pandemonium. "In those few seconds, Peggy," he said, "I knew my dream of a lasting memorial to the South was worth the mental and physical sacrifice it was costing me."

Next day newspapers gave glowing accounts of the affair. One said, "The memorial is now assured. Signed, sealed— ready for delivery to all the generations. . ."

Word of Gutzon's success spread throughout the country. He had already accomplished what artists and engineers had said was impossible and he had only just begun.

No doubt the unveiling of Lee's head had something to

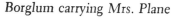

Borglum carrying Mrs. Plane

do with the record-breaking crowd that gathered at Capital Square in Raleigh, North Carolina, to witness the dedication of Gutzon's statue of Governor Aycock on March 13th and the even greater turnout in Chicago when the Sheridan statue was formally dedicated in July.

Gutzon's success at Stone Mountain was undoubtedly the reason Doane Robinson, State Historian of South Dakota, wrote to him about an idea that he had had for a long time for some type of monument to be carved in the Black Hills. "Would it be possible," he wrote, "for you to design and supervise a massive sculpture there?"

"Can't you be satisfied with one mountain?'" asked Mary hopefully.

Gutzon was quick to point out that the difficult engineering problems had been solved on Stone Mountain. "From now on," he said, "mountain carving will be nothing but pleasure."

So, with twelve-year-old Lincoln and his associate Tucker by his side, he went to see the Black Hills. They arrived on September 24, 1924 and by the evening of September 25th, accompanied by Robinson, C. C. O'Harra, president of the School of Mines, and other interested citizens, they had walked or ridden on horseback over about a hundred miles of rugged wooded and mountain area and had climbed to the top of the seven-thousand-foot Harney Peak. Gutzon was wildly enthusiastic. Tentatively he selected two granite spires for carving and before he left the area he had made a hasty drawing of George Washington and Abraham Lincoln to show how they would appear on the spires.

Spurred by the possibility of the Black Hills project, by the success of Lee, and by the fact that the Stone Mountain Confederate Monumental Association was meeting with suc-

Gutzon Borglum (left) working on his design for Stone Mountain, with Smoke as model

cess in fund-raising activities, Gutzon doubled his efforts to complete the head of Jackson. He brought the seven-foot plaster model of Jackson's head from Stamford and he also brought Smoke to pose for the statue of Lee's horse, Traveler. Since more and more of his time was being spent in Georgia, Mary agreed to take Lincoln and Mary Ellis out of school in Connecticut, and move to Georgia. Gutzon sold the New York studio and built a temporary working studio at the base of the mountain.

In addition to the actual work he did on the mountain, Gutzon traveled over the country to make speeches and solicit funds for the project. When the Monumental Association decided to ask the United States Mint to issue a commemorative fifty-cent piece to be sold for a dollar, Gutzon agreeably went to Washington and "sold" the idea to Congress and President Calvin Coolidge. That was relatively easy, but after that he had to make nine different models for the coin before he finally succeeded in getting one that met the approval of the Treasury Department, the Art Department, and the Director of the Mint. It meant countless trips to Washington and to Philadelphia. The first coin was struck on January 21, 1925. The financial problems of the memorial were now well on their way toward being solved.

That same month the Borglums bought furniture and moved into a house near the mountain. While Mary looked forward to the day when they would again live at Borgland, she was glad to be near Gutzon and she rejoiced with him over the wonderful progress of the work. Jackson was all "roughed in" and ready to be finished. The date for unveiling Jackson and Davis was set for Davis's birthday, June 3rd.

Gutzon felt sure he could meet that date. The work on the mountain was going splendidly. True, he was having his troubles with Randolph and other members of the association. Gutzon thought they were spending too much money on routine office affairs and he told them so. On the other hand, they didn't understand the technicalities of carving a mountain, and even though the work was moving rapidly, they felt that Gutzon was neglecting it because he wasn't sitting on the mountain every minute. Mostly Gutzon ignored the association and did as he pleased. He was interested only in getting the memorial carved on the mountain.

In February, Lester Barlow, who had become more and more enthusiastic about the mountain project, came to look over equipment. He had a claim against the United States Government for back royalties on an invention, and told Gutzon that when the claim was settled he would donate one hundred thousand dollars to the mountain. Gutzon accompanied him back to Washington in the hope of helping him to settle the claim.

He had been in Washington but a few days when he received a telephone call from Tucker urging him to return to Atlanta at once. Gutzon knew Tucker was no alarmist, and that something must be seriously wrong. Tucker met him at the station in Atlanta on the morning of February 25th and wasted no time in telling his story. The association had offered him a generous sum to complete the work on the mountain, using Gutzon's models. Tucker said he just turned and walked out of the room without even bothering to explain that he couldn't complete the work even if he wanted to. Actually there was no real model because every day flaws and defects in the mountain appeared that meant constant revamping and changing of the original model, and only Gutzon could make these changes. Tucker went on to say that his refusal had not helped; the members of the association had decided they didn't need Gutzon and were meeting at that very moment to vote him out. Then they planned to turn his models over to stone-cutters who would finish the job.

Gutzon went directly to the mountain. He had to protect his design at any cost. He ordered the stunned workmen to push the plaster casts of Jackson and Lee off the platform onto the rocks below. Then he took Homer, a devoted laborer who had been with the project from the beginning, to the studio, gave him a crowbar, and ordered him to smash the studio model of the central portion of the memorial to bits. Sam Venable, who had joined Gutzon on the mountain, said afterwards that never before had he witnessed such sorrow as Gutzon displayed. Gutzon went from the studio to the home of one of Venable's sisters where Mary was waiting.

He had not been there long enough to find out what was really going on when Tucker came rushing in, grabbed him by the arm, and hurried him into a waiting car. They were barely out of sight when a constable arrived at the house with an order for Gutzon's arrest. Gutzon had destroyed property that allegedly belonged to the Monumental Association.

Next day some of the Atlanta newspapers carried big, black headlines: "BORGLUM FUGITIVE FROM JUSTICE." A year before the same papers had acclaimed the unveiling of the head of Lee with, "The memorial is now assured. Signed, sealed—ready for delivery to all the generations. . ." Columns of accusations against Gutzon were printed. Meanwhile North Carolina had welcomed the so-called "fugitive" with warmth and friendliness. Governor Angus McLean said he would call out the militia to protect Gutzon, if necesary. Needless to say, Georgia's attempt at extradition failed.

Despite all that had happened, Gutzon believed he would somehow be allowed to finish his "dream" for the South. So he stayed with good friends in North Carolina to be close by when Georgia beckoned him. The press throughout the nation and many fellow artists spoke in defense of Gutzon, but the Association turned a deaf ear to any plan of reconciliation. Little old Mrs. Plane, who was ill at the time of the executive committee's action, quietly went to sleep when she was informed of what had happened and never woke up.

On April 16th, the Monumental Association formally ratified a contract with Augustus Lukeman, a New York sculptor who had been born in Virginia, to carve the Stone Mountain Memorial.

Shortly after, Gutzon poured out some of his heartbreak to his good friend Gerald Johnson, who was writing a book about Stone Mountain. "In these months of nightmare," wrote Gutzon, "I have tried to follow Kipling's 'keep your head while those about you are losing theirs and blaming it on you.' But there are days between the stress of things when the world seems numb, inert, and there is nothing left but the will to hold on and it is as with the mother—her child gone, there is no relief."

Gutzon never knew when Lukeman decided to blast his head of Lee off the mountain, nor did anyone else. It was done quietly and behind canvas. Lukeman began his own design, but in 1928 work was abandoned. After that, several attempts were made to recall Gutzon to the work. By then Gutzon was far away and busily engaged in other work, but each time he responded hopefully. However, not until many years after Gutzon's death was work on Stone Mountain resumed, and in 1970, 55 years after Mrs. Plane first discussed the memorial with Gutzon, a carving of Lee, Davis, and Jackson was dedicated.

Mary and the two children joined Gutzon in Raleigh as quickly as they could and the friendly North Carolinians allowed Gutzon to use an empty building on the fair grounds as a temporary studio. Tucker was with him and soon Villa and Homer came too. There wasn't much work for any of them. Villa knew how to make violins and was able to sell a few. This helped financially and also revived an old interest of Gutzon's. Years before he had played the violin, though he was merely an amateur. Now, taking it up again gave him an outlet for some of his pent-up emotions.

Randolph and his henchmen were not content just to leave Gutzon alone. They flooded the country with circulars defaming his character. In Newark, where Lum had had to make excuses for years for the delay in completing the War

Memorial, the circulars had their effect. Gutzon had been unable to get delivery of the bronze castings from Italy and in desperation he sent Villa to the foundry to find out what was wrong. Villa reported back that some of the figures sent as early as 1922 had not yet been cast.

The unveiling had been set for November 11, 1925. It had to be cancelled again and Lum wrote to Gutzon, "I will give no further thought to the subject and forget it, as nearly as I can come to doing that, until someone tells me there is some chance of getting the monument during my lifetime."

"Trust me a little longer," was Gutzon's reply.

The Georgia people sent circulars to the Black Hills, too. Robinson had met Gutzon only once, but he had been impressed by Gutzon's sincerity and his imaginative vision. "I see no reason to change my opinion," said Robinson. Fortunately, after his visit to the Hills, Gutzon had met South Dakota's Senator Peter Norbeck in Washington and had discussed the project with him. Stone Mountain literature that was distributed to the Congressmen didn't change Norbeck's opinion of Gutzon either. In fact, just six days after Gutzon was driven from Georgia, a bill permitting the carving of giant statues in the Harney National Forest became a law. The bill had been passed largely through the combined efforts of Senator Norbeck and Judge William Williamson, United States Congressman from South Dakota. At the same time, Robinson was instrumental in getting a similar bill through the state legislature.

There wasn't any money for the project but that didn't dampen Gutzon's enthusiasm. Mary, who had not wanted Gutzon to take on the burden of carving a second mountain, was now grateful that Gutzon had agreed to do it. She wrote their good friend Herbert Myrick, a Massachusetts publisher,

Gutzon and Lincoln Borglum

"My husband's only salvation in the mental turmoil into which the outrage done to the child of his brain and heart in the South threw him has been to create new visions. Whether or not we lost everything material was as nothing compared to the importance of his keeping his creative powers, and he has kept them, thank God!"

In the summer of 1925 Gutzon had made tentative plans for carving three or four figures—Washington, Jefferson, Lincoln, and possibly Theodore Roosevelt—in the Black Hills, and newspapers began to give publicity to the project. He had already given up the original plan of carving two figures on the two granite spires. In August he and Lincoln went back to the Hills to locate a mountain suitable for carving.

After spending two weeks exploring the hills he decided that Mount Rushmore, a large granite mountain, in a wild, remote section, was the ideal spot. Years before, Charles E. Rushmore, a friendly young lawyer from the East, had scouted the area, checking property titles for a client who was interested in mining. One day he inquired of his guide the name of one of the mountains. "Never had any," was the response, "but from now on we'll call the damn thing Rushmore." The name was officially recognized by the United States Board of Geographic Names in 1930.

Except for a few men of vision, South Dakotans had little or no enthusiasm for the idea of carving a memorial on Rushmore. In fact many were loudly critical. "Whether they like it or not," said Gutzon, "is of no consequence to me. This is to be a national monument. It will belong to all the states. However, it will be South Dakota that will reap the financial reward from the thousands of visitors who will come to view the monument. Too bad the people of South Dakota are too blind to see this."

With enthusiasm and energy that belied his fifty-eight years, Gutzon arranged for impressive mountain dedication ceremonies to take place in October. He returned to the Hills late in September with his photographer Charles d'Emery, and an assistant to help survey and to make accurate drawings of the mountain. On the day of the dedication some three thousand people journeyed over roads that were hardly more than trails to witness the event that was climaxed by a colorful flag-raising ceremony.

Gutzon had been a student of American history all his

Borglum and his assistants carrying the American flag to the top of Mount Rushmore

life. To have the privilege of building a monument symbolizing the growth of American democracy was, to him, nothing short of a sacred trust. He gave a great deal of time and thought to planning the flag-raising ceremony. It was to depict the periods when other nations ruled over the vast territory that has become the United States of America. Six huge flags, eighteen by twenty-four feet, made for the occasion by a group of Rapid City women, were hoisted in rapid succession.

The first, the Bourbon Flag, commemorated French possession in 1743. Then came the flag of the Spanish Empire to
celebrate the transfer of the Louisiana Territory to Spain in
1756, followed by the French Tricolor to commemorate
French possession under Napoleon. To symbolize the transfer of this Territory to the Colonial Republic under Jefferson,
the American flag, showing fifteen stripes and fifteen stars, was
flown. It remained flying while the Lone Star Flag, to honor
Texas, and the Bear Flag of California, along with streamers
for Oregon, Alaska, and Panama were hoisted. Finally the
American flag as of the dedication date, October 1, 1925, was
hoisted. It had thirteen stripes and forty-eight stars.

Actual work on the mountain would have to wait until
some funds could be raised, but in the meantime Gutzon
planned to make models of the carving. Somehow he still
couldn't bring himself to completely abandon hope of being
recalled to Stone Mountain. When the Trail Driver's Association in Texas asked him if he would be interested in doing
a monument for them, he jumped at the opportunity because it gave him an excuse to stay in the South. He fixed
up a studio in an old shed in San Antonio and began the
creation of a monument to the early cowboys who braved all
kinds of hardships to drive their herds of longhorns North.

For a time, Mary and the children went back to Stamford. Mary tried to relieve Gutzon by taking over many of
his problems. It was she who made all the shipping arrangements for the return of the bronze casts of the "Wars of
America" from Italy. This was no small undertaking. In
addition to the delays, there were last-minute, exorbitant
charges. Vignali built a special truck to haul the tremendous
work to the dock. Then he wrote to Mary that the vehicle
was so high and wide that the authorities would not permit

them to use it. "We therefore put eight strong horses to a wagon," he wrote. "They were accompanied by a crew of electricians because in many towns the electric wires had to be removed before the wagon with its giant load could pass." Needless to say, the hundred thousand dollars had long ago been spent in the making and casting of the statue.

On May 30, 1926, five thousand people stood in the rain to witness the dramatic unveiling of the heroic monument in Newark, New Jersey. Faces on the figures are those of actual people. A likeness of Van Horn, the monument's donor, is in the group, and Gutzon and Lincoln are there, representing fathers seeing their sons off to war. At a signal, two giant yellow balloons lifted the flag of the city of Newark from the monument and out fluttered ninety-six carrier pigeons with messages to each state.

The "Wars of America" Monument in Newark, N. J.

Gutzon, who had worked up until the very last minute getting everything ready, was still in his working clothes when he stepped to the microphone to speak. Afterwards, the papers reported that he suffered "mike fright" and had to lay aside his prepared speech. It wasn't "mike fright" at all. It was just that all of a sudden Gutzon was so filled with gratitude that he had been able at long last to keep his promises to his dear friend Ralph Lum, that all he could say was, "It would be impossible for me to express the pleasure and the gratitude to God that I am able today to deliver to you. . .this memorial monument to the people who have founded and protected a new freedom of the world!"

That night Gutzon, Mary, Lincoln, and Mary Ellis drove back to Borgland. Gutzon spoke eagerly of "getting home," which made Mary hope that the big house might again be filled with the laughter of friends and that the two studios might once more be crowded with statues in the making. When they turned down the old Wire Mill Road and approached Borgland, Mary half expected to see Marcelline come bounding to greet them. Then Mary knew she was indulging in wishful thinking. She remembered how she had sobbed all the way home when they had found Marcelline dead in the middle of the road. And she remembered how strangely little Mary Ellis had looked at her and said, "I didn't know mothers ever cried."

"Texas is a wonderful place," Gutzon was saying. "We'll move there and I will commute back and forth to Mount Rushmore until we can get suitable living quarters there."

And Mary answered, as she had so many times before, "I'm ready to go wherever you go, Dane."

Gutzon Scales New Heights at Mount Rushmore

11

LINCOLN SAT quietly beside his father as they drove across the country toward Texas and listened attentively while Gutzon told of his reasons for choosing Washington, Jefferson, Lincoln, and Theodore Roosevelt as subjects for his carving on Mount Rushmore.

Lincoln already knew all there was to know about the techniques of mountain carving. He had been at his father's side most of the time at Stone Mountain. In fact Lincoln had been at his father's side ever since he could remember. He had sat beside his father at dozens of banquets where Gutzon was the speaker of the evening and he had never tired of listening to him. This meant that Lincoln was absent from school more days than he was present, but even so he knew as much about great art, literature, and history as most adults.

Gutzon was at his best when he and Lincoln were together. Lincoln always understood what Gutzon meant without a lot of explanation. "If I can memorialize for the ages a tiny bit of America's greatness by carving four of her leaders who contributed so much to this greatness, then I will have contributed something of value to the affairs of man," said

*Gutzon working on an early model of the heads for
Mount Rushmore*

Gutzon. "You, Lincoln, may one day be asked, 'Why did your father choose these four men?' I'll tell you why. Because I want this memorial to symbolize the creation and the extension of our United States. It must tell the story of the forming of our government and then of the saving of our union. It must also include the story of the completion of Columbus's dream of a water route to India.

"Washington represents our independence; Jefferson personifies 'government by the people' and also by his purchase of the Louisiana Territory he is chosen to portray the growth and expansion of our country; Lincoln preserved the union for us; and Theodore Roosevelt saw, in the building of the Panama Canal, the completion of the dream of Columbus, and he knew the value of the West in the development of our nation.

"I want to create a monument so inspiring that people from all over America will be drawn to come and look and go home better citizens."

Gutzon was silent for several miles, and then he added, "Nothing but the hand of the Almighty can stop me from completing this monument."

Lincoln knew his father meant what he said.

Mary and Mary Ellis had stayed at Borgland so Mary could put the house in order for the time when they would be with Gutzon wherever he decided to establish headquarters —in Texas or in South Dakota. Fortunately, a fine, dependable Irish couple, Mary and James Reilly, lived on the place and looked after things when the Borglums were away.

Ten-year-old Mary Ellis was still remembering some of the ugly, unkind things that had been said to her by classmates in Georgia during the days following the Stone Mountain holocaust. "I wish we could settle down and live in one place like an ordinary family," she remarked as she was packing away some of her "treasures" that were being left behind.

"Would you rather have your father or would you rather have an ordinary father?" quietly countered Mary.

Mary Ellis was suddenly ashamed of herself. She forgot all about Stone Mountain when she remembered all the wonderful, happy times she and Lincoln and her mother and father had had together. She also remembered the extra, special things that her father had done just for her, such as the telegram he had sent her when she was only seven, saying: "My dearest little girl, I will be home Sunday with three new dresses and a hat for you. Love to Mother and Lincoln."

"Let's hurry, Mother," said Mary Ellis, "so we'll be all ready to leave when Daddy is ready for us."

Mary had serious problems to solve before she could leave

Borgland, problems that Mary Ellis knew nothing about. Back taxes were due on the property and the Stamford collector was getting insistent in his demands for payment. In desperation Mary wrote their good friend Myrick for help. After trying to untangle Gutzon's extensive financial obligations, Myrick himself made a substantial payment on the tax debt.

Meanwhile Gutzon and Lincoln were in San Antonio where, in his deserted warehouse studio, Gutzon was finishing the models for Mount Rushmore and working on the Trail Driver's Monument. Some days he dropped other work and turned his attention toward creating a new model of a Confederate Memorial. One late afternoon, after he had worked all day on Lee without even stopping to look at the mail, he asked Lincoln to see if there was any mail that needed immediate attention. In a few moments, Lincoln let out a whoop. "Oh boy, Dad, here's something you'll like!"

It was a request from the state of Georgia asking Gutzon to design a statue of Alexander H. Stephens, vice-president of the Confederacy, for Statuary Hall in the nation's Capitol. Gutzon promptly wired them, "I am honored and delighted to make a statue of Stephens for Georgia."

He made a seated model of the frail, small Stephens, and sent it to Georgia for former Governor N. E. Harris and the committee to approve. Gutzon couldn't take the model himself because there was still an indictment against him and he was subject to arrest if he entered the state. Newspapers reported that tears of emotion filled the former Governor's eyes when he looked at Gutzon's gentle portrait of Stephens. A Georgia quarry sent a block of white Georgia marble to the San Antonio studio and Gutzon put Villa to work on the carving while he, Tucker, and Lincoln went to Rushmore.

Gutzon wired Mary and Mary Ellis to meet them there.

He got to South Dakota first and rented a primitive cabin in the sleepy, all-but-deserted mining village of Keystone, three miles from Mount Rushmore. While some work was being done to improve the road from Rapid City to Rushmore, a distance of twenty-five miles, there was little more than a trail from Keystone to the mountain.

Every day for several weeks Gutzon, Tucker, and Lincoln made the rugged trip to Rushmore and scaled the mountain to take measurements and to make tentative plans for the placing of the faces. It was not a happy time for Mary and Mary Ellis. The cabin, which was little more than a shack, had the most meager equipment. Water had to be carried from blocks away. "But this is only temporary," Gutzon, who

The first measurements are being taken for the head of George Washington on Mount Rushmore

seemed immune to physical hardships, kept assuring them.
Not until he had completely satisfied himself that there
was enough rock at Mount Rushmore for four faces and had
studied the mountain at all hours of the day to determine
the natural lighting effect was he ready to make his first
formal report to the Mount Harney Memorial Association, a
Commission that had been created at the time the state had
authorized the carving. Governor Carl Gunderson, who was
opposed to the entire project, was ex-officio chairman. Norbeck, fortunately, was vice-chairman. Gutzon's report indicated that each face would be proportioned to a figure four-
hundred and sixty-five feet tall—the faces would be sixty feet
from chin to forehead.

With the report completed there was no reason for the
Borglums to stay in South Dakota, so in September 1926,
Mary, Mary Ellis, and Lincoln went to Borgland.

There was not a penny available with which to begin the
carving, but Gutzon wasn't discouraged. Armed with fine,
artistic photographs of his models, taken by d'Emery, Gutzon
toured the big cities, giving speeches and calling on wealthy
businessmen. He didn't raise any money, but he did get a lot
of good newspaper publicity for the project. One bit of publicity that helped arouse interest among businessmen of South
Dakota appeared in the Dakota Farmer, one of Myrick's pub-
lications. It gave a detailed account of the memorial and
carried a picture of Gutzon's model of the Washington head
on the cover.

The outlook for the Rushmore Memorial at the beginning
of the year 1927 was bleaker than it had been at any time.
There was no money and no prospect of getting any. John
Boland, a Rapid City businessman who had been born and
raised in the shadow of Mount Rushmore, was deeply inter-

ested in the project and was doing everything he could to encourage local business associates to contribute financially, but
by March he had been able to raise only nineteen hundred
dollars. Norbeck, Williamson, and Gutzon were working in
Washington on the possibility of securing a federal grant, but
so far the only progress that had been made was the nod of
approval given to Gutzon by Secretary of the Treasury Andrew
Mellon to an appropriation of two hundred and fifty thousand
dollars if the same sum could be raised elsewhere. Mellon
said he would support such a measure if it were brought before
Congress.

With the possibility of federal help in the offing, Gutzon
insisted on having some kind of formal contract. Up to this
time he had given freely of his creative abilities and his own
money simply because of his faith in the monument and in
the sincerity of Norbeck and Robinson. Since there wasn't
any money actually available for the project, the contract was
nothing more than a formality, but it did make Gutzon feel
better. The contract, as drawn up by Norbeck, Williamson,
and Myrick in Washington, D.C. on March 1, 1927, gave
Gutzon the responsibility for the artistic excellence of the work
and provided for paying him an honorarium when funds were
in hand. Gutzon wanted Tucker to have a part in the project,
too, but Tucker, who by now had established a business in
Florida, was willing to come only if he could have a salary of
ten thousand dollars a year. It seemed like a lot of money to
the Committee but, on Gutzon's recommendation, they finally
agreed to give Tucker a contract providing for the salary
he wanted.

Until Norbeck and Williamson got some congressional
action on federal support, nothing could be done, so Gutzon
moved his family from Borgland and took up temporary resi-

dence in the Menger Hotel in San Antonio. Gutzon was already referring to Texas as his adopted home. He liked the big open spaces and he liked the mild winter climate. He had grim recollections of the Connecticut winters when he had worked in the bitter cold on the "Wars of America."

"We'll spend our winters in Texas and our summers in the Black Hills," said Gutzon to Mary. Then, as an afterthought, he added, "Maybe in the spring and fall we'll go to Borgland."

In her heart Mary was sure Gutzon did not intend to live again at Borgland, but still he didn't want to part with it even though it was a constant drain on his financial resources. "Maybe, somehow, some day, we will go back and walk again in the woods and recapture all the beautiful dreams we had," mused Mary.

Gutzon was planning a sightseeing trip to get better acquainted with Texas when news reached him that President Calvin Coolidge intended to spend his summer vacation in the Black Hills. Norbeck, Williamson, Myrick, and the recently elected Governor William J. Bulow of South Dakota had been extolling the beauties of the state to the President for months. Early in 1926, Francis Case, the enthusiastic young editor of the Hot Springs *Star* had wired Williamson urging him to use his influence to bring Coolidge to the Black Hills for his vacation. Ever since Case had climbed the mountain in 1925 to participate in the "flag-raising" dedication and had listened to Gutzon's inspiring description of a monument grand enough to honor the United States, he had been an ardent supporter of the enterprise. Gutzon, too, had been in touch with the President but Coolidge had shown little enthusiasm for the idea. Now that he had decided to go to South

Dakota, Gutzon was happy. "This is what we need to get things moving," he said.

Gutzon was right. Soon after the President's plans were announced, fifty thousand dollars had been raised.

On June 5, 1927 the President moved into his summer White House—the Game Lodge in Custer Park, only a few miles from Rushmore. A few days later Gutzon and Tucker arrived, hired some help, and went to work. "I'll bet my father didn't suffer any more hardships when he crossed the country with a wagon train in 1864 than we're having now," said Gutzon. There was only a wagon trail part way from Keystone to the mountain. The remainder of the way was little more than a footpath so the dense forest had to be cut before a team could get through with the heavy equipment. Even then much of the equipment had to be carried by hand up the steep slope. Timber also had to be cut away before the power line could be put up. A well had to be dug to provide drinking water for the workers and a stream dammed to provide water to cool the compressors.

Within a month, though, stairways and scaffolding were on the mountain and compressors and drills were being tested. After all, Gutzon and Tucker were old hands at conquering mountains.

August 10th was the date set to celebrate the first drilling on the mountain. On that day Coolidge came by car from the summer White House to Keystone. The remainder of the way had to be traversed on horseback and Coolidge had dressed for the occasion. He wore cowboy boots and a ten-gallon hat. The President appreciated the salute given him: twenty-one stumps were blasted to make way for the building of a road to Rushmore.

President Calvin Coolidge, accepting one of the first drills to be used on Mount Rushmore

"We have come here today to dedicate a cornerstone that was laid by the hand of the Almighty . . ." said the President. ". . . the people of the future will see history and art combined to portray the spirit of patriotism." When the President finished his talk he handed Gutzon some drills and Gutzon climbed to the mountain top. He was lowered over the cliff in a saddle seat by Tucker to drill the first points for the face of Washington. No tight rope walker had ever given a crowd a greater thrill. They roared with excitement. The program concluded when Gutzon presented one of the four drills he had used to President Coolidge, one to Norbeck, and one to Robinson, keeping one for himself.

A few weeks later, on August 31st, Gutzon took part in another celebration in the Black Hills that was almost as exciting to him as the "first drilling" on the mountain. It was the dedication of the Camp Coolidge Boy Scout Retreat. Daniel Beard, beloved National Scout Commissioner who had contributed so much to the founding of the Boy Scouts of America, was scheduled to be the speaker, but at the last minute he was unable to come. Gutzon, who had many times voiced his belief that the future of America lay in the hands of her youth, was proud to take Beard's place on the program. President and Mrs. Coolidge and their son John sat on the platform with Gutzon and the Scout officials. "Every American boy ought to want to be President of the United States," said Gutzon, "but when he develops and finds his real work that work may be even more important than being President. The important thing is that every American youth should want to add something worthwhile to some part of our national life."

Gutzon went on to tell the boys about his great dream of carving an American memorial on Mount Rushmore. "The American memorial," he told the Scouts, "will be a record of the labor and sacrifice of men who were all once boys, who had their ideals and whose ideals developed into an integral part of the nation we now have."

Afterwards President Coolidge told Gutzon, "You were a real inspiration to those boys."

"It is the other way around, Mr. President," said Gutzon. "Those boys, and others like them all over America, give me the inspiration I need to try to find and release the faces of four great Americans within that granite mountain."

Actual drilling to find those faces began on October 1st. By then winches had been installed on top of the mountain and other equipment was ready. A cableway had also been in-

Workmen going down Mount Rushmore in harnesses

stalled to carry supplies and tools from the canyon to the top of the mountain. The workers, for the most part, were miners. They had to be taught the ways of mountain carving.

Gutzon bought an old log house on Grizzly Creek, next to the road leading to Rushmore, to use for a studio. He had his big five-foot model of Washington's head sent from San Antonio. That eight-hundred-pound head was quite a sight as it went bumping over the rugged road in a truck from Rapid City to the studio.

Gutzon sent Lincoln to San Antonio to bring back his model of the faces on the mountain. This first model showed only the heads of Jefferson, Washington, and Lincoln. On the return trip Lincoln skidded off the road, the little model flew out of the car, and the car turned over on it. When a passing motorist stopped to ask Lincoln if he needed help and if anyone was hurt, Lincoln replied, "No, thank heavens, only the mountain is cracked. The presidents are okay."

When Lincoln finally reached South Dakota and Gutzon learned of the accident, he was so thankful that Lincoln hadn't been hurt that he showed little concern over the crack in the mountain. "A broken mountain is much easier to repair than a broken boy," was his comment.

Gutzon decided that the contour of the mountain was such that the use of the projector to transfer his designs to it would not be practical. He worked out a complicated system of coordinated circles, degrees, and plumbobs for enlarging the heads mechanically. With his system of "pointing," the high points of the faces were first located and marked on the mountain. By constantly making new measurements or "points" the stone could be removed from the faces by dynamite and by drilling to within two or three inches of the finished head. Aside from the sculptor, the pointer was the most important man on the job.

It was the last few inches of stone that Gutzon intended to use to give the figures life and character. When the carving reached the final stages. Gutzon would treat the mountain as if it were a chunk of marble in his studio and take off the stone a little at a time to achieve just the effect he wanted.

When the work at Rushmore was well under way Gutzon left Tucker in charge and hurried back to Texas to complete a "rush order." Coolidge was planning a visit to Cuba and Cuba wanted three busts for display when he got there— Theodore Roosevelt, William McKinley, and Leonard Wood. Gutzon had only thirty days to complete the modeling of all three. It gave Gutzon special pleasure to do Roosevelt and Wood since he had known these two men so intimately.

He finished just in time to take his family to Washington to witness the unveiling of his statue of Alexander Stephens in Statuary Hall. A delegation of dignitaries from Georgia, including some members of the Stone Mountain Association came.

"The Stone Mountain affair seems to have been completely forgotten," remarked a friend to Mary.

"It will never be forgotten," was Mary's curt reply. "At least not by Gutzon."

Before the Borglums returned to Texas Gutzon visited the Civil War battlefield at Gettysburg, Pennsylvania. His good friend Governor McLean of North Carolina had written him that the state wanted a tribute to its soldiers to be placed at Gettysburg and he asked Gutzon to submit a design. Gutzon was guided on an extensive tour of the field by Mrs. E. S. Lewars, a writer who was well-versed in the three-day battle of Gettysburg. Gutzon was already familiar with the history of the Civil War, but after he had tramped for hours over the Gettysburg battlefield he told Mrs. Lewars, "Your minute description of the hour-by-hour events on this bloody field have given me a real feeling of the part played by the North Carolina soldiers and I will be able to design a better memorial because of your help."

By the end of January Gutzon's proposed monument had

Borglum at work on his model for the Gettysburg memorial statue

been approved by the North Carolina committee. His completed model shows four figures: a mortally wounded officer on his knees points the way to the others; an infantryman, both hands gripping his Remington rifle, is in the lead; close beside him is a younger foot soldier, followed by a flag-bearer. The color bearer's face was modeled from an old daguerreotype of Orren Randolph Smith who designed the flag.

Gutzon signed a contract to deliver the heroic-sized bronze statue at a total cost of fifty thousand dollars in time for dedication July 3, 1929—the sixty-sixth anniversary of the culmination of the battle.

Work continued on Mount Rushmore until the early part of December, 1927, when it was shut down because of sub-zero weather. The money was all gone, too, but Tucker reported that rock had already been removed down to the point of Washington's eyes. Gutzon was pleased with the progress that had been made in such a short time and predicted that in 1928 Washington would be completed. Early in the year Tucker, at his own expense, assembled a skeleton crew at Rushmore so he would be all ready to start drilling as soon as funds were available. With Coolidge's blessing on the project and his support assured, Gutzon was certain federal funds would soon be forthcoming. In May, Norbeck succeeded in getting a bill passed in the Senate authorizing two hundred and fifty thousand dollars of federal money if an equal amount could be raised from private contributions. But there were delays in getting the measure before the House and finally Tucker, greatly discouraged, had to release his men and close down the work.

Fortunately Gutzon had work to do in Texas and was able to direct his energies to the completion of the Gettysburg monument.

Nevertheless, he did complain to Norbeck now and then about the lack of interest on the part of South Dakota's citizens. Norbeck would have been glad of contributions from his constituents, but he knew it was hard for farmers who were struggling to hold onto their land to get enthusiastic about a carving on a mountain. "You have to try to understand that not all men are blessed with the vision and imagination that you have," he told Gutzon.

Meanwhile, Gutzon's services as a sculptor continued to be sought. Arizona wanted a statue of General John Greenway in Statuary Hall and his widow, Congresswoman Isabella Greenway, promptly recommended Gutzon. She visited Gutzon in San Antonio. "He wouldn't let me leave until I had told him my husband's entire life story. After that he studied the photographs and examined the clothing of General Greenway that I had brought. He seemed to develop the most amazing insight into the character of the General. I know Mr. Borglum will make a wonderful statue," said Mrs. Greenway to members of the Arizona Committee.

With commissions literally pouring in, Gutzon's San Antonio studio became inadequate, even though he had moved from the warehouse to a larger room in a machine shop. For weeks Gutzon combed the city to find a more suitable location. He had about given up when, walking one day with Lincoln in picturesque Brackenridge Park, he spotted an abandoned old stone pumphouse. "What a fine place for a studio!" he said.

"But Dad," said Lincoln, "it's in a public park and it belongs to the city." Gutzon didn't even hear Lincoln.

"It's a sturdy structure," said Gutzon. "Made of Texas limestone. I can have it in shape for a studio in no time at all."

And "in no time at all" he secured the permission of city

authorities to remodel the structure, drew plans, and then stood over the workmen while they repaired doorways and windows, put in a skylight, and added an ell. At the same time, while he was in a remodeling mood, and since he now intended to spend much time in Texas, he arranged to have three rooms at the Menger Hotel redecorated for permanent living quarters.

A little stream ran under the studio building and there was a trap door in the floor. Lincoln liked to sit and look into the hole. Once in a while he would see a baby alligator. Sometimes snakes crawled into the studio and draped themselves on the plaster figures. Once a squirrel ate the nose off General Greenway and Gutzon had to give him a new one. All in all, though, it was a fine studio and Gutzon was so grateful to the city of San Antonio that every Sunday afternoon he opened the studio to visitors. Many visitors came back week after week to watch the progress on the Gettysburg memorial or to admire General Greenway or the fine, sensitive features of Sidney Lanier, Georgia's famed poet and musician, whom Gutzon was immortalizing for the Washington Memorial Library in Macon. When Major Gordon W. Lillie, known as "Pawnee Bill," came to pose for his bust, the studio was filled with children who came to see Buffalo Bill's old show partner.

Texans showed little or no interest in a work which Gutzon had done purely as an expression of his own passion for liberty and justice. It was a bronze bas relief plaque on which were molded the profiles of two rather ordinary looking men. But the message that was written beside the faces wasn't so ordinary. It read: "What I wish more than all in this last hour of agony is that our case and our fate may be understood in their real being and serve as a tremendous lesson to the forces of freedom so that our suffering and death will not have been in vain."

The two faces on the plaque were of Nicola Sacco and Bartolomeo Vanzetti, Italian emigrants who had been arrested in Massachusetts in 1920 and charged with the robbery and killing of the paymaster and guard of a shoe factory in South Braintree, Massachusetts. The men were tried and sentenced to death. The defense claimed there had been insufficient evidence and many people throughout the country, including Gutzon, shared this view. Applications for re-trial were denied even after a confessed criminal gave evidence that the killing had been done by a bandit gang. Sacco and Vanzetti were executed on August 23, 1927. Gutzon was firmly convinced that the men had been unjustly executed and he made the plaque in the hope that Massachusetts would one day review the testimony, convince itself there had been an error, and erect the tablet in Boston. The tablet was never placed and long after Gutzon's death it mysteriously disappeared from the old studio at Borgland where it had been put.

Before the year was over Gutzon was on a half dozen civic committees in Texas and had taken on tasks ranging from designing an outdoor theater for San Antonio to beautifying the waterfront at Corpus Christi. In Corpus he was welcomed by Mrs. Lorine Jones Spoonts, a leader in civic affairs. She was already trying to promote a movement for systematic planting of palm trees along the barren streets of Corpus. The Borglums toured the state with Mrs. Spoonts and Gutzon discussed the street and highway beautification project with Chambers of Commerce groups and women's clubs.

Gutzon enjoyed the friendly hospitality of the Texans and he made many friends. In Beeville, Texas, he often stopped for a real Texas meal with Mrs. Spoonts's brother, A. C. Jones,

a well-known cattleman, and his wife. Gutzon helped Mrs.
Jones plant shrubs on the school and court house grounds
and palm trees along one of the streets. Louella, one of the
Jones's pretty daughters, wasn't much interested in tree planting but she thought Lincoln was wonderful, so she often went
along on the planting expeditions. She was the same age as
Mary Ellis and Lincoln thought they were both "silly."

To redecorate Texas on the scale Gutzon envisioned was,
in itself, a full-time job for an ordinary person. For Gutzon,
it was just part of his civic duty. This, coupled with all the
commissions he had, plus Mount Rushmore, should have been
enough to keep him occupied. But when he heard from Sam
Venable that there was a flicker of hope that Stone Mountain
might be revived, he dropped everything and braved arrest to
go to Georgia to talk to Venable. It was a wild goose chase
but the "let-down" was somewhat softened by a letter from
Ignace Paderewski that awaited him on his return to Texas.

"My dear great Friend," began the letter, which was written
in longhand even though Paderewski had writer's cramp and
wrote with difficulty. ". . . During my hard fight for Poland
you showed me a great deal of sympathy and the memory of
it I shall always cherish. . . . As you well know, I am a Pole
and as a Pole I want to ask you now a very great favor. A group
of my compatriots have decided to erect in the city of Poznan
a monument to the memory of Poland's most generous bene-
factor, President Wilson. . . . My decision is: the statue of
that great American should only be done by the greatest
American artist, by the greatest living sculptor in the whole
world. I now take the liberty of asking you whether you are
willing and free to do in Poland for Woodrow Wilson what
Thorwaldsen did about a hundred years ago for Copernicus?"

Gutzon replied, "My dear, dear friend, Paderewski: You

Drawing of Ignace
Paderewski by Borglum

can never know how much happiness your letter gave me. It is wonderful of you to turn to me. I shall have a real chance to serve a man I have always loved. What a pleasure! What a fine historic note! Think of it!"

In his pleasure to serve Paderewski, Gutzon completely forgot that at one time he and President Wilson had been anything but "dear friends."

There were a hundred questions Gutzon needed to ask the Committee and arrangements would have to be made to have the statue cast in Europe. Gutzon considered going to Europe but the Rushmore legislation might be passed at any time and he wanted to be ready to start work the moment money was available. So Mary and Lincoln went to Europe to visit Paderewski and to make the necessary arrangements. Mary Ellis was in boarding school in Texas and was having a fine time. Her roommate was her new friend Louella Jones.

Gutzon began at once to design a statue of Woodrow Wilson while he waited impatiently for news of the federal appropriation for Mount Rushmore.

Faces Emerge on the Mountain

12

On George Washington's birthday, February 22, 1929, the long-delayed bill for federal funds for Mount Rushmore was approved. In addition to providing funds, the law also provided for the creation of the Mount Rushmore National Memorial Commission—twelve presidential appointees, an executive committee of five, and a paid secretary. The Commission superseded the old Mount Harney Memorial Association. John Boland, who had actively sought local financial support for the project, was one of three South Dakotans appointed by President Coolidge. Other members were wealthy, influential business leaders from all parts of the country. Gutzon was especially pleased at the appointment of several of his good friends, including Mrs. Spoonts and Joseph S. Cullinan, a Texas oil man. Two vacancies remained for President Herbert Hoover to fill when he took office in March. He appointed Williamson and another South Dakota Congressman, Royal Johnson.

Gutzon was anxious to begin work, but President Hoover failed to call a meeting of the Commission. Finally, toward the end of May, Borglum decided to pay Hoover a visit. His reception was not especially cordial, and the President refused to be hurried.

Gutzon had no intention of leaving Washington, however, until the Commission did meet. Meanwhile Mrs. Wilson put a room in her house at his disposal so he could examine and sketch some of President Wilson's clothing. For Paderewski's sake, Poland was going to have the best statue of Wilson that Gutzon could create.

The President called the meeting on June 6th. Cullinan was elected Chairman of the Commission and Boland was named Chairman of the Executive Committee. The following day the Commission put in a requisition to the United States Treasury for $54,670.56 to match the funds raised by private subscription that had already been spent on the mountain.

Gutzon immediately wired Tucker to resume work. A second meeting of the Commission was set for July 17th and Gutzon wanted activity on the mountain to be in full swing when the new Commission met at Rushmore.

Borglum, who now had an agent to handle his many requests for lectures, had several speaking engagements to fulfill before that time. He also went to Gettysburg to oversee the placing of his North Carolina Monument. He supplied a touching, dramatic climax to the unveiling ceremonies on July 3rd, when he arranged for an airplane to fly low over the battlefield. As it dipped its wings in tribute to the soldiers of North Carolina, roses were scattered over the field from the plane.

The new Commission assembled for its second meeting in Gutzon's newly constructed log cabin studio located on Doane Mountain, a prominence east of Mount Rushmore. Even the most hard-headed of the businessmen was stirred as he stood in front of the big picture window, gazed at the face of Washington that was just beginning to emerge, and listened to Gutzon dream aloud.

Gutzon's log
cabin studio

"Think, if you can, of faces the dimensions of a five-story building carved on a mountain peak where clouds fold about them like a great scarf and the moon hides behind a lock of hair," said Gutzon. "If I can discover these faces of Washington, Jefferson, Lincoln, and Roosevelt within this mountain, they will, according to geologists, remain to tell the story of America for the next five million years."

"If you can do such a thing," remarked one of the commissioners, "what a legacy you will leave to America!"

With a few minor changes the Commission accepted Gutzon's contract that had been drawn with the old association. However they thought ten thousand dollars a year was too much for Tucker. Late in August, Tucker resigned. He was disgruntled over the reduction in pay and because his back salary and money he had advanced to keep the work going were paid so slowly.

Gutzon and Tucker had been through a lot together and Gutzon was truly sorry to see him go. However, after Tucker left, Borglum claimed that in his efforts to stretch the meager funds, Tucker had cut corners that might affect the safety of the workers, such as putting improper rails on the stairway and on scaffolding. With Gutzon, the realization of his dream always came first; he was quite willing to repudiate his friends if he thought it necessary.

J. C. Denison was appointed to replace Tucker. He was capable, but lacked his predecessor's years of experience. This meant Gutzon would have to spend more time at the mountain. "I'm buying a ranch near Rushmore," Gutzon wrote Mary in San Antonio. "Looks like we'll be spending a lot of time here for the next few years."

Gutzon had a good time remodeling the buildings on the ranch. He had never lost his passion for balconies and the high ceiling in the little ranch was all the encouragement he needed. He put a decorative balcony at the end of the living room opposite the fireplace. He made a fine guest house out of the old log chicken house. The interior was plastered and French doors and windows added. His greatest joy, though, was in remodeling the barn for a studio. He designed a magnificent huge fireplace. "Looks awful big to me," said one of the workmen.

"I don't like anything puny," was Gutzon's reply.

Work on the mountain and on the ranch was proceeding at top speed when Gutzon returned to Texas to finish Wilson and Greenway and send them off to be cast in bronze. Mrs. Greenway was so pleased with the statue of the General for Statuary Hall that she ordered one to be placed in Arizona.

In all this time, Gutzon had been too busy to submit any plans for the Corpus Christi bay front, though it was two years since he had talked about it with Mrs. Spoonts. He had no definite contract, but was anxious to do something special. He said, "I have many plans for Texas, but I believe the beautification of Corpus Christi is my favorite project." He made a ten-foot plaster model of his plans, and, to stand on the breakwater, designed a colossal statue of Christ with outstretched hand, as if "stilling the waves."

By the end of the work season at Rushmore most of the

available money was gone and the Commission met in Chicago to discuss the financial problems. Gutzon was determined to dedicate the Washington face on July 4, 1930, and this meant funds would have to be available so work could be started again early in the spring. He finally persuaded the Commission to allow the Committee on Design and Publicity to publish an illustrated Mount Rushmore booklet and to sell advertising space in the booklet. The Commission also organized a Mount Rushmore Memorial Society to help raise funds and to help with the improvement of the grounds around the monument. Memberships in the Society, which sold at one hundred dollars each, were to be limited to five hundred. Both enterprises were successful and by spring over twenty thousand dollars had been raised. This fund was matched by the federal appropriation and work was resumed on the mountain.

Over the years Gutzon had witnessed the unveiling of a hundred or more of his own works. He had had a part in planning many of the ceremonies. When he was planning the dedication ceremonies for the Washington face, an associate said, "Don't you ever get tired of dedications?"

"I never unveil one of my works that I do not think of the mother as she presents to the world one of her children for the first time," replied Gutzon. "The world little realizes the anxiety of the creator at this moment. No," said Gutzon, "I never tire of dedications. How could I? Every dedication is a brand new experience."

With his usual imagination and vigor he made the ceremony on July 4, 1930 a memorable occasion for the twenty-five hundred visitors who had traveled over the new graded road and gathered around the log studio on Doane Mountain for the event. Chairman of the Commission Cullinan

Head of George Washington on Mount Rushmore

presided and in his opening remarks he said, "The authority of the Congress to carve colossal portraits of these great men in the granite of the Black Hills has created a perpetual shrine for political democracy."

Fred Sargent, who later became chairman, was also on the platform and as he sat admiring the grandeur of Washington he noticed a small figure climbing down over the nose of Washington. "Who is that?" he said to Borglum.

Gutzon promptly sent a messenger to see who was being lowered over the mountain in the saddle. Within a few minutes the boy was back. "It's Mr. Sargent's little girl, sir," he said.

"Don't worry," said Gutzon to the agitated father, "my daughter has been doing it for years." Nevertheless Sargent never took his eyes off Washington until he saw that his daughter was safely over the top.

Mrs. Spoonts was among the members of the Commission who attended the unveiling. Her niece Louella Jones came with her from Texas and afterwards Louella joined Mary and Mary Ellis on a trip to Canada and a visit to Borgland.

The cheering from the dedication had hardly died down when Boland announced that the treasury was empty and, on July 26th, he ordered the work on the mountain stopped. Gutzon was furious at the Commission for not raising money and Boland because of what he termed Boland's "picayunish" method of handling funds. Boland was no dreamer. He was a firm, methodical business man and he held a tight rein on the finances of the Commission. He could not understand what Gutzon meant when he said, "I have a certain contempt for money, feeling that weighed in the balance with an idea it amounts to almost nothing."

When no funds were forthcoming from the Commission, Gutzon donated money himself and the work was resumed in the middle of August and continued until November, 1930.

Meantime Denison resigned as superintendent and Gutzon replaced him with William S. Tallman who had been on the mountain almost from the beginning. Gutzon sent for Villa to come and help. Matty Reilly, one of James Reilly's sons who had grown up at Borgland, came to try his hand at mountain work.

Charles d'Emery, the photographer, was a frequent visitor to the mountain. He was as enthusiastic as Gutzon about the project. Gutzon carried a small plaster head of Abraham Lincoln in his pocket and as he talked he often took it out and rubbed his hands over Lincoln's rugged features. D'Emery admired the little face and one day when he was leaving the mountain to return to his studio in the East, Gutzon handed him the Lincoln. "Here," he said, "you appreciate him as much as I do."

Right after the work stopped for the winter the Commission met to decide how to raise funds for the next year. The federal appropriation was lying idle because matching funds were not available. Gutzon wanted to hire a professional fund-raiser but the Commission refused. Nobody, however, had any better ideas and finally some of the members of the Commission bought additional memberships in the Memorial Society and Fred W. Sargent subscribed five thousand dollars so there would be enough to begin work in the spring. They also authorized Gutzon to prepare another brochure in the spring.

Gutzon had a number of projects in Texas to look after so the Borglums went south for the remainder of the winter.

In Texas, Gutzon completed designs for a contemplated outdoor theater in Brackenridge Park. Gutzon had no commission to do this. The ladies in charge had no money, but they had to have plans before they could sell the city officials on the idea. Gutzon, who was always interested in doing whatever he could to promote any of the arts, gladly performed the service. He was chairman of the Parking Committee for the State Highway Department and also served on street and road beautification committees in several towns. In this connection, he made a number of speaking tours throughout the state trying to encourage the citizens to do more planting.

In February Gutzon went to New York to inspect the bronze statue of Wilson at the foundry and to arrange for the shipment of the statue to Poland where it was to be un-

Borglum working on clay model of statue of Woodrow Wilson, commissioned by Paderewski for Poland. Charley Johnson, a studio helper, is in front of the statue

veiled in July. Mary and Lincoln had been unable to make satisfactory arrangements to have the Wilson statue cast in Europe when they had gone to visit Paderewski the year before.

While Gutzon was in New York he received a request

from Paderewski, who was then on concert tour in the United States, to meet him to discuss final plans for the placing of the Wilson statue. Paderewski always traveled in a private train car. Oftentimes, when the car was standing in the freight yard, dozens of railroad workers gathered beside the tracks to enjoy a free concert while Paderewski practiced for his evening performance. Gutzon, accompanied by Mary and Lincoln, met Paderewski's train at Abilene, Texas. The Wilson problems were quickly settled, but when it was time for the train to pull out, Gutzon and Paderewski were having such a wonderful time talking together that Gutzon decided to ride along for awhile. Mary and Lincoln went back to San Antonio. Gutzon didn't return home until the next day. He and Paderewski had talked until the early morning hours.

In April Gutzon went back to Rushmore to lay out the work for Tallman and Villa during his absence in Poland. He wanted Washington to be finished to the waist and eight drillers were put to work on Jefferson, at the left of Washington. He also left instructions for blasting away stone on the other side of Washington to get ready for the face of Abraham Lincoln.

Gutzon asked his good friend Francis Case, who was now editor of the Custer Chronicle, to take over the editing of the new brochure. Case was one of the few South Dakotans outside the members of the Commission who sincerely believed in the monument. "For all time to come," he wrote in one of his editorials, "South Dakota will be getting dividends from Mount Rushmore."

At the close of school Mary, Mary Ellis, and Lincoln went to Stamford so Mary could make financial arrangements for the trip to Europe. The Borglums sailed on the afternoon of June 6th on the S.S. Brittanic for Copenhagen to visit the ancestral home of Gutzon before going to Poland. Gutzon waved jauntily to the Statue of Liberty. "I have a feeling, old girl," he said, "that the giants on Mount Rushmore will outlive you by a million years or so." He turned to his stepsister Anna who was accompanying them on the trip. "I used to envy Bartholdi his creation of Liberty," he admitted, "but I don't any more."

Gutzon was at home at once in Denmark. He spoke an ancient dialect that he had learned from his father as they jogged over the Nebraska countryside with a horse and buggy. In the far north of Denmark they visited Borglum Cloister which was famed in the Middle Ages as a monastery and educational center. One of Gutzon's forbears named Niels Sorenson Mothe had been a monk there and after the Lutheran religion became the State religion he married. Later, by Royal Mandate, members of the family were commanded to take the name of the Cloister their ancestors had served. Gutzon found a worn tablet buried in the floor of the great chapel with the name "Borglum" still discernible.

"Look carefully," he said proudly to Lincoln and Mary Ellis. All their lives they had heard their father tell stories of Borglum Cloister, but only now did they really appreciate their ancestry.

On their return to Copenhagen, the Borglums were presented to King Christian. His Majesty called attention to the fine portrait bust of his grandfather that graced a gilt mantel. "You are a fine sculptor," he said to Gutzon. "We are proud of this statue."

Then he conferred upon Gutzon the decoration of the Order of the Dannebrog, given for outstanding service to Denmark. It was a beautiful white enameled gold cross suspended by a white ribbon with a red border.

The Borglums reached Poznan a few days before the unveiling of Wilson, in time for Gutzon and Lincoln to oversee the placing of the statue. Gutzon was cutting a map of Poland into the granite platform on which the statue stood when a workman accidentally overturned a can of red paint and it spread ominously across the map. It cast a spell of gloom over the workmen as well as the crowd that had gathered to watch Gutzon at work.

At the last minute Paderewski, who had been in political exile from Poland for some years, decided that his homeland might suffer if he came for the unveiling, so he stayed away. While the dedication was an impressive one, attended by a large delegation from America, including President Wilson's widow and Bernard Baruch, Gutzon was too saddened by the absence of his friend to enjoy the occasion. An even sorrier note was added a few years later when Hitler's troops marched into Poland, tore down the statue, and made ammunition out of it.

On Gutzon's return, he discovered that Villa had cut too deeply into Jefferson's forehead. Villa and some of the other workers had long felt that Gutzon was entirely too cautious in his use of dynamite—that much time could be saved by using larger charges. "Can't they understand that once rock is blasted away it is gone forever. I can't take any chances," said Gutzon. He discharged Villa, but only Lincoln understood that there was a good reason for it.

Lincoln was to enter college in September. He hadn't said much about it because he didn't know whether he really wanted to go or not. At nineteen, he hadn't decided what he wanted to study, because he had given little thought to his future. Gutzon didn't give Lincoln much help or encouragement. In fact, he all but ignored Lincoln's coming departure.

Borglum directing work on Washington head

When Villa left, Gutzon had the excuse he had been looking for to keep Lincoln by his side. "I could use your help right now," he said to Lincoln. "Maybe you wouldn't mind postponing school for a while."

Lincoln found it easy to forget about college in the warm glow he felt at being needed by his father. He went to work on the mountain at once. "I can't ask the Commission to pay you," said Gutzon. "At least not until you're a qualified worker." Lincoln wasn't interested in pay. He was working to help Gutzon. But later, when Lincoln really wanted to go to college, he had become so experienced in the work on the mountain, that Gutzon declared he could not spare him.

In the fall Mary Garden came to sing a benefit concert in Rapid City to help boost the treasury of the Rushmore Commission. She was one of the first to drive over the mag-

nificent scenic road from the Game Lodge to Mount Rushmore that had been designed and constructed on Iron Mountain through the efforts of the beauty-loving Senator Norbeck.
Through carefully planned tunnels, along a winding highway, Mount Rushmore could be viewed as if it were in a
huge picture frame. The highway was known as the Iron
Mountain Road but out of gratitude to Miss Garden the
State Park Board approved the Memorial Commission's request to rename the road "Mary Garden Way." When Doane
Robinson made the announcement at a luncheon in honor of
the great star she was so touched she cried.

In 1932 America was in the depths of a depression. No
one—not even the members of the Commission—was willing
to contribute toward mountain carving. Gutzon appealed to
Hoover without success. Norbeck finally persuaded Warren
E. Green, who was now Governor of South Dakota, to release fifty thousand dollars of the unemployment relief fund
for use at the mountain. The money had to be used as wages
for those most in need. Since most of these people were un-
skilled, it was not possible to do much more than improve
the grounds around the base of the mountain where visitors
gathered.

During the year, the Borglums made several trips to San
Antonio. Gutzon was trying to get Corpus Christi to take
action on his bay front plan and he still wanted very much
to do the Christ statue for them. He spent considerable time
in Washington trying to get federal funds for Texas projects.

Early in the year he had been awarded a commission by
the William Jennings Bryan Memorial Association to do
a statue of the Great Commoner. Gutzon was well qualified
to make this statue. He had known Bryan for years and had

once made a plaster cast of Bryan's hand clasping Mrs. Bryan's hand. Gutzon made a trip to Lincoln, Nebraska to visit Governor Charles Bryan, brother of William Jennings, to discuss the statue and to secure the loan of the elder Bryan's flowing cape.

During the time Gutzon was in Washington trying to get funds for Rushmore and working on Texas legislation, the Corcoran Art Gallery allowed him the use of a room for a studio. That's where he made the first model of Bryan.

Later Governor Bryan came to the ranch studio and posed for the large model. Gutzon portrayed Bryan with his right hand upraised and his index finger extended as if he were uttering his famous words, "You shall not crucify mankind upon a cross of gold!" The unveiling of the statue in Potomac Park in Washington, D.C. was attended by President Roosevelt and many other dignitaries, including a delegation from Nebraska headed by Governor and Mrs. Bryan. In 1960 the statue had to be removed from its place in the Park to make way for an approach to a new bridge, but in 1961 the National Park Service authorized the loan of the statue to Salem, Illinois, William Jennings Bryan's birthplace.

The year 1933 saw no great progress on the mountain. Gutzon spent most of his time refining the Washington face. Bianco, who had been with Gutzon at Borgland and at Stone Mountain, came to help. He became Gutzon's chief carver on the mountain.

Faithful Norbeck had been able to get the relief funds of the year before matched by the already appropriated federal funds or there wouldn't have been any work in 1933 at all. President Roosevelt put Mount Rushmore under the jurisdiction of the National Park Service in the Department of the

Interior but the only difference it made was that some of the bookkeeping details had to be passed on by the Service.

The face of Jefferson was causing Gutzon more and more worry. Villa's mistake had meant that the entire head had to be set back. Gutzon was afraid there wasn't enough stone to do this and still allow for shifting in case cracks or flaws appeared in the granite. By the end of the year Gutzon reluctantly decided to shift Jefferson to the other side of Washington, and the following summer the partially finished face was blasted off the mountain.

In 1934 work was late in getting started, again for lack of money. By March, Gutzon was so disgruntled that he went to Washington to see what he could do to help Norbeck get federal funds for Rushmore. Gutzon also had another project he wanted to promote in Washington. He, along with Mayor William Shaffer of Corpus Christi, was trying to get a Public Works Administration loan to carry out the bay front beautification project. Gutzon was so eager to see the completion of this dream for Texas that he offered to finish his thirty-two-foot statue of Christ "stilling the waves" and to present it to the city without charge when the bay front project was completed.

While Gutzon and the Mayor were busy in Washington, opponents of the plan were busy in Corpus Christi spreading a rumor that Gutzon was seeking to burden the city with a tremendous debt to rehabilitate the bay in order to have a suitable spot to display his statue. Mayor Shaffer strongly defended Gutzon, saying, "Mr. Borglum has asked nothing, has sought nothing for himself for all the services he has rendered this city." Nevertheless, as a result of the conflicting factions in Corpus, the Works Progress Administration shelved the application for the loan.

Fortunately the Rushmore project met with greater success. Norbeck, after much wrangling, got the Senate to approve the appropriation of the remaining funds in the Rushmore allotment even though there were no private funds to match it. With the help of Congressmen Kent Keller and Theodore Werner and Congresswoman Isabella Greenway, the bill passed the House. When the work started at the mountain, Lincoln, who under his father's tutelage had become familiar with all phases of the work, was put on the payroll for the first time.

Rushmore got a great deal of free publicity in 1934 when the Hearst newspapers sponsored a contest for a six-hundred-word history to be carved on Mount Rushmore. An inscription had been part of Gutzon's design for a long time. At one point he had asked Coolidge to write the inscription but he and Coolidge disagreed over the wording so nothing came of that. Eight hundred thousand entries were submitted in the Hearst contest and many cash prizes were given. No entries were ever used because eventually Gutzon abandoned the inscription idea in favor of a great Hall of Records to be cut in the stone of the canyon behind the faces. Gutzon felt that records carved or placed in a room in the mountain would last much longer than any identifying inscription on the surface of the mountain.

The constant struggle for appropriations was a source of real irritation to Gutzon. In the spring of 1935 he again went to Washington to build up interest and support for Rushmore among his friends in the Legislature. "One hundred and fifty thousand Americans came to view the half-finished monument last year," Gutzon told his good friend Senator Alben Barkley, "and yet there are still those who claim Mount Rushmore is not a national project." Gutzon had a lot of friends in Washington, including President Roosevelt, who had always been friendly toward the Rushmore project. Gutzon's influence, coupled with Norbeck's ingenuity in handling legislation, and the cooperative help of Senator Bulow and Representative Theodore Werner, resulted in a new, outright appropriation of two hundred thousand dollars, with no stipulation requiring private funds.

Gutzon ordered the men to the mountain in June. The work continued until November. By then Jefferson was clearly discernible to the right of Washington. Abraham Lincoln had begun to emerge from the rock too.

Visitors came at the rate of three thousand a day. Frank Lloyd Wright was one of the most enthusiastic. "The noble countenance emerges from Rushmore as though the spirit of the mountain had heard a human prayer and itself became a human countenance," wrote Wright in an appeal to encourage others to visit the work.

Many of those who came climbed the five hundred steps to the top of the mountain to get a first-hand view of the work. Here on top of the heads was a tiny village. There was a shed to shelter the workmen from sudden rains, another to house the tools and the dynamite, and one on top of each head to house the winches. The sole duty of the winch operator was to turn the wheel of his winch to lower or raise the worker who had been let down over the side of the mountain in the saddle seat. A "call boy" sat on the side of the mountain and relayed the desires of the workers to the operators. Later, when there were more workers on the faces, a speaker system was installed in the winch houses so they could hear the "call boy" over the noise made by

Call boy on Mount Rushmore

the drills. There was a small studio on the mountain too to house Gutzon's five-foot model.

Visitors were amazed at the life-like appearance of the giant figures at such close range. Workmen looked like pygmies walking across Washington's eighteen-foot lower lip. Oftentimes two men worked in one of Jefferson's eyes at the same time. Gutzon's knowledge of the use of natural light for effect on statues was the result of a lifetime of study. Once an old lady asked him what kind of paint was used to make Jefferson's eyes so blue. "There is no paint," he said kindly. "I just sprinkled a little bit of sun in each eye."

It was an awe-inspiring sight to see those faces emerging from that craggy old mountain. Lincoln, who was doing more and more of the "pointing," was often at work on top of the heads taking measurements with a bar and plumbob when visitors were there. He heard them say time and time again, "What a great tribute to America!!"

"If the lawmakers and the bureaucrats and the skeptics could spend five minutes here," mused Lincoln, "maybe then they would see why Dad has to finish this monument!"

Gutzon's Legacy to America

13

On August 30, 1936, Mary Ellis, standing beside her father, looked toward the mountain and gently waved an American flag. Fifteen hundred feet above, on top of Rushmore, Lincoln saw the signal and pressed a button. A cloud of gray dust rose over the mountain, followed by a tremendous boom as huge chunks of granite roared down the mountainside. Three times the jar of a dynamite blast shattered the silence and then the seventy-foot flag that was draped over the mountain swung away to reveal the face of Thomas Jefferson. At almost the same moment a plane circled overhead and little parachutes, each bearing a flag and a chip of granite from the mountain, floated down among the three thousand spectators. Gutzon turned to the President of the United States and said, "I want you, Mr. President, to dedicate this memorial as a shrine to democracy."

President Franklin Roosevelt, who had taken time from his tour of the Great Plains drought area to view the monument, had indicated that his visit was to be an informal one and that he did not wish to make a speech. Gutzon was so sure the President would want to speak when he saw the patriotic monument that he had gone ahead and arranged

Head of Thomas Jefferson nearly completed

President Franklin D. Roosevelt speaking at dedication of Jefferson head

a ceremony, even though Jefferson was still a long way from being finished.

As Gutzon turned to the President, Robert Dean, manager of the Rapid City radio station, moved toward Roosevelt with his microphone. The President's secretary, Marvin McIntyre, plainly angry, pushed Dean aside. "The President doesn't want to speak," he muttered.

The President, who had been gazing intently at the mountain, said, "I've changed my mind, Mac, I must say something." Dean moved forward with his microphone and the President began to speak: ". . . This can be a monument and an inspiration for the continuance of the democratic republican form of government, not only for our own beloved country, but, we hope, throughout the world. . . ."

It was a great day for Gutzon and for Rushmore. In these moments of inspiration Gutzon could forget all about the difficult problems that had to be met daily. Only a few days before the President's arrival a freak accident had put the entire crew in an uproar. It was a murky, cloudy day but there was no rain on the mountain. In Keystone, however, quite a storm was raging. All of a sudden there was a tremendous burst of lightning! It struck a power line in Keystone that led to the mountain. The shoes were blown right off the feet of one of the "powder monkeys." Two other men received shocks. Fortunately none of them was permanently injured and Gutzon, in his anxiety for his men, suffered more than anybody.

Gutzon didn't mince any words when a worker made a mistake and sometimes he even bawled out the wrong person. But he thought of them as his family. Most of them had a fierce loyalty toward him and the same ones showed up for work year after year. Even Villa came back when Gutzon wrote that he needed him. A year or so after Villa had been discharged, Gutzon had visited Villa's studio in San Antonio, and the two old friends had become reconciled.

Gutzon often fired his secretary, Jean Philip, but she always showed up the next day and she was the first to jump to his defense if anybody said anything against him. Jean had been with him since 1933 and Gutzon depended on her more than he realized.

Right now Gutzon was having his problems with the National Park Service. For the first time since the mountain had come under its jurisdiction the Service was taking an active interest. There was an allotment of one hundred thousand dollars for Rushmore in this year's annual budget and they wanted to see how it was being spent. They sent Julian C. Spotts out to the mountain as a resident engineer to relieve Borglum of some of the routine tasks connected with the efficient operating of the equipment. At first Gutzon thought it was a good idea. Spotts saw to it that the bucket lift to the top of the mountain was converted to carry the workmen as well as the tools. Gutzon had been trying to get this done for a long time. He was so excited about the new lift that he sent for d'Emery to "come out and get some good pictures of my new mountain elevator." When the lift was all set to make her maiden voyage d'Emery handed Gutzon his camera, climbed in the cage, and said, "Now you take my picture."

The happy relationship between Spotts and Gutzon was short-lived. Spotts, like Boland, was a methodical man. He was highly critical of some of the makeshift methods and equipment that were being used to carry out the mechanical aspects of the job. "Maybe some of it looks pretty inefficient to him," growled Gutzon, "but if he'll just take a look at

Charles d'Emery standing on **Lincoln's** *chin*

what we've done with no money and makeshift ways, he might change his tune."

But it was the administrative problems that caused most of the conflict between Gutzon and Spotts. Spotts was a conscientious worker and he took seriously his responsibility for having an accurate record of the work at Mount Rushmore. Routine procedure of the National Park Service required outlines of operations, job classifications, reports of progress, and other records. It was Spotts's job to see that these regulations were complied with. Gutzon had no patience with regulations. "I'd choke to death on all that bureaucratic red tape," he stormed. "A million years from now who is going to care how many hours it took to carve Teddy Roosevelt's mustache."

Despite conflicts, much was accomplished during the 1936 work season. Enough stone had been removed for Gutzon to say with certainty that there was sufficient rock for all four faces. Besides detailed work on the Washington, Jefferson, and Lincoln faces, Roosevelt had been definitely located between Jefferson and Lincoln and granite had been blasted to within about five feet of Roosevelt's nose.

In his desire to finish the memorial Gutzon hadn't forgotten Texas. Many times he made the long drive from South Dakota to attend meetings. As early as 1933 he made suggestions, drew designs and created interest in Texas for the celebration in 1936 of her hundredth year of independence from Mexican rule. But he was not awarded a single commission out of forty awarded to build monuments for the celebration. Gutzon had met with other disappointments in Texas too. So far, nothing had come of his dreams for beautifying the bay front at Corpus Christi. His big statue of Christ was still unfinished. The Trail Driver's Monument was only a plaster model in a museum. After approving Gutzon's plans for an open air theater, San Antonio discarded them in favor of a local architect's plans. After a particularly disheartening visit to the Lone Star State Gutzon wrote a friend, "I am leaving Texas for good., I have had nothing but disappointments here."

On his return to Rushmore, Gutzon devoted time and energy to the creation of new statues. He delighted many members of the Rushmore Commission with his expressive portrait busts. Families of the commissioners were especially grateful to Gutzon. "Imagine my surprise when returning from a walk last evening to find the fine bust of the Senator standing on the table," wrote Mrs. Norbeck. "I am overwhelmed with such a magnificent gift."

Gutzon and Senator Norbeck often disagreed but they both loved beauty and they had a deep admiration for one another. Gutzon was deeply saddened when Norbeck passed away at the end of the year. "Mount Rushmore and South Dakota have lost one of their truest friends," he said.

The controversial Thomas Paine was the latest character to take form in the ranch studio. Gutzon had been commissioned by the French-American Thomas Paine Memorial Commission, which was headed by former premier Edouard Herriot, to complete the eight-foot statue in time for an unveiling in France on the 29th of January, the two-hundredth anniversary of Paine's birth. With work on the mountain closed down, Lincoln did much to help his father get the plaster cast ready to be sent to France to the famous foundry of Rudier where it was to be cast in bronze and coated with gold.

Gutzon was looking forward to the Paine dedication with more than his usual enthusiasm because Helen Keller, who had a deep sympathy for the much-maligned author of *The American Crisis*, was going to participate. Gutzon arrived in Paris several days ahead to oversee the casting of the statue. There were delays at the foundry and the Committee encountered difficulties in their negotiations with the French Government so at the last minute Gutzon had to wire Miss Keller, who was in England, that the ceremony had been postponed. He invited her and her companion, Miss Polly Thomson, to come to France anyway and attend a dinner on the 29th in memory of Paine, and they accepted.

Gutzon was touched by Miss Keller's greeting. "Meeting you," she said, "is like a visit from the gods. I admire you not only because you are a great artist, but also because you think greatly through your marbles. When skill and daring imagination meet a masterpiece is born. In your statue of Thomas Paine you are preaching anew the liberty that shall reshape civilization."

When Miss Keller expressed to Gutzon a long-cherished desire to visit the Rodin museum and touch the Rodin masterpieces, Gutzon quickly responded with, "Tomorrow, if you wish, I will go with you to the museum and show the masterpieces to you."

Next day Gutzon secured the permission of the Department of Beaux Arts to allow Miss Keller to touch the statues. At the museum Gutzon led Miss Keller first to Victor Hugo. Her hands gently descended from the great forehead over the cheeks and the nose and the beard and then she spoke of the trouble she sensed within the mighty man. She moved reluctantly from Hugo to Balzac and on to Clemenceau. Her hands played over the bowed head of *The Thinker*. "What loneliness must have enveloped the first thinker as he reached toward the unknown!" she exclaimed. She lingered and lingered over *The Hand of God*, and at a statue of a figure bent in desperation, she said, "He is weeping in my hand."

That evening Gutzon wrote to Mary. "I shall never forget that soul-stirring hour with Helen Keller."

There were delays and delays over Paine and long after Gutzon returned home he was still trying to get the statue placed. Then the Nazis came and Gutzon didn't know what ill fate had befallen Paine. The story came to light long after Gutzon's death. For some unknown reason, the storm troopers who raided Rudiers did not push open the dusty, cobweb-covered door to the little room where Paine was stored, and when the war was over Rudier found Paine right where he had been left. On January 29, 1948, the gilded statue was unveiled in a park opposite the American building of the City University.

On Gutzon's return from France, the Borglums took a trip to California to look at a house that a friend was offering for sale in Santa Barbara. Gutzon had made up his mind he wanted to spend his last years in California where he had first begun his career as an artist. The Santa Barbara hacienda was set in the middle of a beautiful garden. Gutzon took an option on the place at once and wrote his dear friend Frank Lloyd Wright, "I've bought a home in California. This will be my last home. The studio will be about an eighth of a mile from the house set in a beautiful grove of oak, Japanese bamboo, and pine. In fact I want two studios at least forty feet by sixty feet one opening into the other."

Gutzon was seventy years old but he planned for the future as if he were just embarking on his career. He hadn't changed much over the years. He had the same shaggy mustache and he'd been bald ever since he was a young man.

Gutzon Borglum when he was 70 years old

Lately he had taken to wearing a silk scarf all the time and on him the scarf seemed right. His eyes had dimmed a bit and he wore a pair of *pince-nez* on a black silk ribbon hung around his neck.

Gutzon went to Washington and Mary, Lincoln, and Mary

Ellis stayed on for awhile in California. Gutzon's Rushmore contract was about to expire and he wanted to arrange a new one. As usual, he had trouble. His old contract called for a twenty-five per cent honorarium on the total amount spent per year on the mountain. He wanted an increase of five per cent and he might have gotten it but Boland was bitterly opposed and fought it. So the new contract carried no increase in pay. Then Secretary of the Interior Ickes didn't approve it until November, so it was well into 1938 before Gutzon received his 1937 pay.

Gutzon's friend Francis Case was now a Representative in Congress and it was he who went before the appropriations committee and extolled the value of the memorial to the nation. Congress was reluctant but they finally appropriated fifty thousand dollars for work in 1937.

Gutzon's family returned from California in time for Lincoln to begin the mountain work in April. Efforts were directed to roughing in Roosevelt and to doing fine finishing on Lincoln preparatory to the dedication on September 17th, the one hundred fiftieth anniversary of the adoption of the Constitution. Visitors who climbed to the top of the mountain were amazed to see how Gutzon had put highlights in Lincoln's eyes with jutting pieces of stone the size of a small room. A mole on Lincoln's face was sixteen inches across.

Judge Williamson, now Chairman of the Commission, presided at the dedication and Senator Edward Burke of Nebraska was the principal speaker. Five thousand came from all parts of the country to witness the unveiling, including Frank Lloyd Wright. The famed architect had first visited the monument in 1935 and had been so deeply impressed that in 1936 he had brought his entire Taliesin Fellowship group to tour the Black Hills.

Mary Ellis's good friend Louella Jones came from Beeville with her aunt Mrs. Spoonts for the occasion. When it was time for Mrs. Spoonts to return to Texas, it was Lincoln who suggested that Louella "stay around awhile." Lincoln took her all over the mountain. She thought it was great fun to go over the side of the mountain in a saddle seat. She liked to ride up and down in the aerial cage even though she knew that earlier in the year something had given way just before a carload of men reached the top and the carriage had gone speeding down. The men had quite a jolt before they stopped it with an emergency brake. One man jumped and was seriously hurt, but came back on the job as soon as he recovered. That and the lightning episode were the closest anybody ever came to being killed in all the time it took to build the monument.

The Borglums headed for Santa Barbara as soon as the weather got too cold for the men to work on the mountain. In all but the severest weather the workmen could be kept warm by the use of a wood-burning stove on scaffolds covered with tarpaulin. It was usually lack of money rather than cold weather that caused the stopping of work in wintertime.

On the way to Santa Barbara the Borglums spent three days with William Randolph Hearst amidst the rare treasures that overflowed his fabulous home, San Simeon.

At Santa Barbara Gutzon rested in the warm California sunshine and drew designs for his new studio. "It will have a balcony and a big fireplace," he told Mary. "I ought to be getting it started. I could be doing a lot of work here in California if I had a studio." Mary didn't say anything. She knew Gutzon had forgotten all about the legal difficulties that had to be settled with the owner of the house before the Borglums could even buy the estate.

When Gutzon wasn't dreaming over a new studio he was trying to dream up a way to get Rushmore away from the National Park Service. The past year had been one long conflict. Gutzon's main complaint was that he was not allowed to proceed with the carving without interference, maintaining that he was the only one qualified to say what should be carved and when. Officials of the National Park Service who had to face Congressional Appropriation Committees and try to give answers to such questions as: How much more is the monument going to cost? How long will it take to complete it? had a difficult task. Once A. E. Demaray, Associate Director of the National Park Service, who had not been able to get any kind of financial estimate or long-range work schedules from Gutzon, appeared before a committee and made the remark that "with the very temperamental sculptor in charge of the work, not knowing what he may change, or may not change, it is quite a difficult thing for us to give an accurate estimate or one that we ourselves would want to stand back of."

Gutzon, of course, had no way of knowing just how much stone would have to be removed before, as he put it, "this or that head would emerge," and he was furious at being called "temperamental." He wrote a scathing reply to the press but it went over the desk of a timid editor and afterwards Gutzon confided to a friend, "They took all the bones out of my story and the poor little thing limped into print like a sucked gum drop."

"I'll have to get a new Commission with new powers authorized by Congress," Gutzon said to Mary. "There would be nothing to keep the President from appointing some of the members of the present Commission to a new Commission, and he could leave off some of the members, too. That is if he wanted to," Gutzon added. "I'll also have to get a big enough appropriation to carry the work. I actually think I have enough friends in Washington to get the job done."

"Why don't you try, then?" said Mary.

So in the spring Gutzon went to Washington once more.

Lincoln went to Rushmore to open the work season but not before he and Louella Jones from Beeville, Texas had slipped off to be married. In his spare time, Lincoln built a house for himself and Louella right next to his parents' ranch home. He also took down the little old log cabin on Grizzly Creek where Gutzon had worked on the first models of Rushmore and rebuilt it on the ranch.

In Washington, Gutzon told his troubles to all his friends. Many of the legislators had, by now, been to Rushmore and had been impressed by what they had seen. For the first time, Gutzon appeared before a Congressional Committee to discuss the Memorial. Gutzon was a good talker, and he spoke convincingly of the need for a new Commission and for more funds to carry on the work.

Gutzon's friend, Congressman Case, told his colleagues, "Every doubt and every question will melt into nothingness if you will visit Mount Rushmore and see the Memorial itself."

Gutzon was in the balcony on the day the bill, which included a three-hundred-thousand-dollar authorization and provision for the appointment by the President of a new twelve-man Commission with full authority to proceed with the work, came up before Congress. One bill after another that had to do with monuments and parks was defeated. Gutzon began to feel tired and beaten. He left, went to his hotel room, and started to pack. The phone rang.

It was Case. "What happened to you!" he asked.

"I've worked too hard," Gutzon said. "I just couldn't stay and see Rushmore defeated."

"But the bill passed!" shouted Case.

Gutzon had his appropriation and Mount Rushmore was no longer under the supervision of the National Park Service. Under a new Commission appointed by President Roosevelt, which did include five members from the old Commission, the work on the mountain proceeded peacefully. Financial matters were handled by the Treasury Department. Gutzon had a little trouble here, too, with red tape, but at one point he wrote to George W. Storck, the Treasury Department accountant responsible for Rushmore funds, "I may write you very frankly about some things that are disturbing me for the moment, but I beg of you not to take me too seriously." In fact, Gutzon later wrote, "I never had any real trouble with the Treasury Department or with the National Park Service."

Except for a few weeks, the work continued throughout the entire winter of 1938-39 with sometimes as many as thirty men on the mountain at one time. Most of the work was concentrated on finishing the Roosevelt face for unveiling in July, 1939. Gutzon began construction of a much-needed large studio to replace the old log one. Visitors overran the old studio until Gutzon literally had no room at the mountain to make necessary adjustments on his models.

Gutzon also began removing stone for the Hall of Records. He was determined there would be a place in the mountain where important records of our civilization could be preserved for posterity. "The four faces on Rushmore will endure as long as these granite mountains remain and the story of these faces should also be preserved," he said.

From time to time friends urged Gutzon to carve his signature on the mountain. He scoffed at the idea. "Who put the faces there is of small importance in the scheme of things. It is enough that they are there."

Gutzon asked Frank Lloyd Wright to help with the design of the Hall. "Now, the question before us," he said, "really is whether we could work together—each yield to the other the points of importance in the general structure. I don't want the Hall to be a modern, blocked affair. I want it rich in color, rich in form, and reminiscent of American culture."

Wright promptly answered, "So glad to hear from you, old boy. Somehow I like you well enough to give you anything you want. I have an idea you need me, in a way, and it would

Entrance to Hall of Records in a small canyon behind the faces. The Hall was never completed

be fun to see how happy we could make you. Let me know when you are ready to go."

In April 1939 there was much family rejoicing when Mary Ellis married David Vhay, a young architect whom she had met in Santa Barbara.

Then in May, Gutzon suffered a real blow. In a reorganization program, President Roosevelt ordered the Monument returned to the administration of the National Park Service effective July 1st. Gutzon made a hurried trip to Washington to appeal to the President to rescind his order, but Roosevelt remained firm.

Gutzon returned to Rushmore unhappy and disgruntled, but he still planned with enthusiasm for an elaborate program for the unveiling of the Theodore Roosevelt face on July 2, 1939. The celebration was held in conjunction with South Dakota's fiftieth anniversary. Twelve thousand visitors took part in a colorful program that included Indian music and singing and dancing. The four faces were lighted at night with the sparkle of fireworks and with floodlights. Gutzon and eighty-three-year-old Doane Robinson were probably the proudest two men in the world that day. Fifteen years had passed since they had first shared a dream for a monument on a mountain in the Black Hills.

After the dedication, one of the spectators, an autograph collector, wrote Gutzon about a letter of Theodore Roosevelt's that he had bought at an auction in which Roosevelt said, "If a monument is ever built to me, I hope Gutzon Borglum does it."

In accordance with the President's order, responsibility for the work on the Memorial was now split among the Commission, the Treasury Department, and the Park Service. Construction was immediately halted on the new studio and on the Hall of Records. The Park Service and some members of the Commission felt that the four faces should be completed before consideration was given to any additional work. Gutzon poured out his feelings to his friend Wright and told him not to make any definite plans about the Hall of Records.

"You are a sorry old warrior—all scarred up and bleeding grandly," Wright answered. "I hope some day we can do something."

But nothing more was ever done on the Hall of Records.

Even though Gutzon had many disagreements under the new organization, work on the mountain continued to progress. Lincoln was now superintendent at Mount Rushmore and he relieved Gutzon of all petty details. Gutzon devoted his time to refining the features of the four faces.

Gutzon also had time to give more and more thought to the Confederate Memorial, a subject that had never really

The Trail Driver's Monument

Mary and Gutzon Borglum with their daughter Mary Ellis and her son, their first grandchild

been out of his mind since February 25, 1925, the day he had destroyed his models and fled from Atlanta. In fact, there had been talk again of reviving the project, and Borglum had made several trips to Atlanta during 1939. Early in January 1940, he wrote his dear friend Mrs. Elizabeth Tucker Mason, one of the heirs of Stone Mountain, "Happy New Year and love to you! 1940 must mean a complete revival of Stone Mountain and the revival of the public's and the Nation's interest in it." Later in the year he visited Atlanta again and again but his dream for a monument to the valor of the South remained as far from realization as when he had first conceived the idea in 1915.

Nevertheless, the year 1940 had its compensations. On April 10th, Mary Ellis presented Gutzon with his first grand-child, named David Lincoln.

Gutzon rejoiced a bit, too, when Texas finally decided to

cast his Trail Driver's Monument in bronze to place in front of the new Trail Driver's Memorial Building in Brackenridge Park. But he had no interest in tending to the details of getting the cast made. Lincoln was the one who went to Texas, made the mold from the model in the Witte Museum, and packed and shipped it to the foundry to be cast.

These days Gutzon seemed to enjoy doing busts. He was a little weary of colossal works. Early in the year he had gone to Rochester, New York, and spent two weeks in a hotel room modeling the bust of his good friend Frank Gannett, owner of a newspaper chain. Right now he was working on a bust of Thomas Brackett Reed, a former United States Senator from Maine. The bust was to be placed in the nation's Capitol.

In the late summer Gutzon went to Washington to appear again before a Congressional Committee to seek additional funds for the Memorial. The three-hundred-thousand dollars that had been appropriated in 1938 was nearly gone. Gutzon estimated that he would need sixty thousand dollars to complete the faces, eighty thousand for the Hall of Records, and ninety-five thousand for a great stairway to the Hall. Congress reluctantly appropriated eighty-six thousand dollars, which was to be used to complete the heads.

Shortly after his return to Rushmore, Gutzon spent one of the most rewarding days of his life. On September 14th he took two thousand Boy Scouts on a guided tour of Mount Rushmore and saw for himself the impact of his great patriotic work on young Americans. The Boy Scouts of Region 10 were holding their annual meeting in the Black Hills and the visit to Rushmore was one of the high spots of their three-day outing. In the afternoon the boys heard Dr. James E. West, Chief Scout Executive, tell them of his determination to make scouting something "that will insure the idealisms conceived

Head of Theodore Roosevelt on Mount Rushmore

in the time of Washington, fortified at the time of Jefferson, preserved through the wisdom and leadership of Lincoln, and exemplified through the life of Theodore Roosevelt."

The boys gazed at the face of Roosevelt that Gutzon had draped with a flag to honor him as one of the great Boy Scouts.

Then it was Gutzon's turn to speak. He thought of the Boy Scouts he had spoken to in 1927 when Camp Coolidge had been dedicated, when the four faces were still deep in the mountain. "Yes," he thought, as he looked out over those young faces, "it is the youth of America who inspired me to complete this gigantic task."

The boys stood silent and solemn. "Men of tomorrow," Gutzon began. "It was thirteen years ago that I stood just back of that pine tree, facing President Coolidge as he dedicated this great rough cliff on which I had promised to carve a monument to our philosophy of government." Gutzon went on to tell the story of the monument. "Sixty feet high those heads are, five hundred feet above where we stand. I am carving them so you will understand them and so your children's children will understand them."

A day or so later Melvin Munger, Scout Executive, Black Hills Area Council, wrote Gutzon in a letter of appreciation, "The talk you gave and the trouble you went to in making arrangements for the program did much to make a success of what Chief West refers to as a history making conference."

Gutzon had always been in demand as a speaker, but now that the four faces on Mount Rushmore were a reality, civic organizations throughout the country were eager to hear the story of this gigantic undertaking told by its creator. The story, of course, wasn't quite finished. There was still refining work to do on the faces and the Hall of Records was hardly begun, but it was a pretty good story even without an ending and Gutzon told it well.

Toward the end of January 1941, Gutzon made preparations to be gone from the mountain for several weeks on a speaking tour of the Middle West. Mary was going along. She liked to listen to Gutzon talk and he liked having her in the audience. Gutzon would soon be seventy-four years old but that didn't stop him from climbing over the faces and preparing detailed instructions for Lincoln to carry out in his absence.

Lincoln drove Mary and Gutzon to the train. Gutzon was in a jovial mood. Louella was expecting a baby and Gutzon was already bragging about "my second grandchild." Lincoln waited on the platform until the train was out of sight. He felt strangely sad and lonely. "I wish Dad hadn't gone," he said when he got home to Louella.

A month later Mary called for Lincoln and for Mary Ellis, who was then living in Reno, Nevada, to come at once to Chicago. Gutzon had had a minor operation and suddenly had taken a turn for the worse. Lincoln and Mary Ellis came at once to Chicago, but in a few days Gutzon was gone. He died March 6, 1941. Lincoln had promised his father a number of years before to have him buried in California, but at the time of Gutzon's death the family was in such a state of shock and confusion that arrangements for immediate burial in California presented insurmountable problems. So Gutzon was temporarily laid to rest in a crypt in a Chicago mortuary.

The day of Gutzon's death, Russell Arundel, Chairman of the Commission, proposed that his body be entombed at Mount Rushmore. Representative Case introduced a bill in Congress to authorize the burial. President Roosevelt signed the bill on July 11th. The cost of the tomb was to be borne by funds privately subscribed. Mary was not enthusiastic about burial at Rushmore. She said there had been too much unhappiness for Gutzon there, and she, as well as Lincoln and Mary Ellis, felt they should respect Gutzon's wishes for burial in California.

Not until 1944, however, were arrangements finally completed for the removal of Gutzon's body to Forest Lawn Memorial Park, Glendale, California. Borglum was entombed in the Court of Honor as an "immortal," on November 14, 1944, in the first service of its kind to be held there. A memorial tablet at Gutzon's grave is inscribed with the following tribute by Rupert Hughes:

> "His birthplace was Idaho. California first taught him art. Then France, who first gave him fame. England welcomed him. America called him home. His genius for the exquisite as for the colossal gave permanence on canvas, in bronze, in marble, to moods of beauty or passion, to figures of legend and history. Nations, cities, colleges paid him tribute. As patriot he stripped corruption bare. As statesman he toiled for equality in the rights of man. At last he carved a mountain for a monument. He made the mountain chant: 'Remember! These giant souls set America free and kept her free. Hold fast your sacred heritage, Americans! Remember! Remember!' "

In 1955, Mary Borglum was laid to rest beside him. She had spent the intervening fourteen years trying to pay a lifetime's accumulation of debts and writing the story of Gutzon's life.

Lincoln Borglum in his father's studio looking up at models of the four heads. Through the window can be seen the actual heads on the mountain, nearly complete

Lincoln completed the work on the mountain for which his father had left instructions. The last bit of work was done on October 31, 1941, A total of $989,991.32 had been spent on the Mount Rushmore Memorial.

Anna Mary, the second grandchild Gutzon had awaited so eagerly, was born on April 23, 1941. Lincoln and Louella nicknamed her Robin and as soon as she could toddle around she was climbing on the mountain with her father, who was still Superintendent.

Gutzon hadn't quite finished the bust of Senator Reed

and he hadn't left any instructions for finishing it. Lincoln didn't need any instructions. His father had been instructing him to be a sculptor all his life, but never once had he asked him to try his hand at sculpturing. So Lincoln hadn't. But now he finished the bust.

In September 1941, the National Park Service assumed complete responsibility for the Memorial. The Mount Rushmore National Memorial Society, which had been organized in 1930 primarily as a fund-raising project, remained active and has continued to give its support to the monument. John Boland, whose interest in the monument had begun when Gutzon paid his first visit to the Black Hills in 1924, continued to serve the monument as President of the Society until his death.

Lincoln continued as Park Superintendent until 1944 when he and Louella and Robin moved to Beeville, Texas, where Gutzon's fourth grandchild, James Gutzon, was born. The third grandchild had been a girl born to Mary Ellis on October 16, 1944. Mary Ellis and David named her Diana Borglum Vhay.

There's not much in Texas to show for all the plans and dreams Gutzon had for the big state, but in Beeville, years after his father was gone, Lincoln could still point with pride to palm trees and shrubs planted in the early thirties by Gutzon. Lincoln's children weren't impressed. They wondered why their grandfather, who carved a mountain, would bother about a few trees and bushes for a little town like Beeville. Robin and Jimmy took more pride in a statue in a little cemetery on the edge of town. It is a gentle, quiet statue of Christ done by their father.

Corpus Christi never did do anything about Gutzon's statue of Christ "stilling the waters," but when Francis Case,

Above: Lincoln Borglum with his father's clay model of Christ with upraised hand; Below: Lincoln Borglum's own statue of Christ at Beeville, Texas

now a Senator, proposed that a figure of Christ be placed
high on a mountain overlooking the site of the Passion Play at
Spearfish, South Dakota, a few miles from Mount Rushmore,
Josef Meier, portrayer of the Christus, suggested that Lincoln
finish Gutzon's statue for this purpose. In completing his
father's statue, Lincoln put a little more gentleness into the
facial features to suggest Christ as a teacher in the Sermon
on the Mount. He also changed the fingers of the outstretched hand to suggest an invitation, "come unto me,"
rather than "stilling the waves" on the Sea of Galilee as
Gutzon had planned when he designed the statue for Corpus
Christi.

At Mount Rushmore, under the watchful care of the
National Park Service, the grounds around the Monument
have been cleared and landscaped, parking lots have been
enlarged, and additional tourist facilities constructed. The
sheds on top of the heads were long ago removed. The steps
up the mountain rotted away, so visitors are no longer permitted to climb to the top. But Park Rangers are on the
grounds to tell the story of the four faces and there's an
amphitheater where, in the evenings, the story is told and
illustrated with slides to show how the great Memorial was
built. In 1950 floodlights were installed to illuminate the
faces at night.

In 1959, largely through the efforts of Senator Case,
President Dwight D. Eisenhower reestablished the Memorial
Commission to work with the Park Service to erect a suitable
memorial to Gutzon Borglum at Mount Rushmore. In addition to Senator Case, among those appointed by the President
to serve on the Commission was William Williamson, who
had been an ardent supporter of the Memorial since its inception. Also appointed were the widows of three men who

had served many years on previous Commissions—Peter
Norbeck, John Boland, and Paul Bellamy. Russell Arundel
was renamed Chairman. Lincoln Borglum was named to
the Commission and Conrad Wirth, Park Director, also
agreed to serve. Other members named were Senator Karl
Mundt, Senator John G. Townsend, Representative E. Y.
Berry, and Sterling Ely. The Commission met in the summer of 1960 at Mount Rushmore to discuss plans for the
proposed memorial to Gutzon Borglum and Lincoln and
Conrad Wirth were named to work out detailed plans. The
Commission also considered the possibility of moving Gutzon's body to Rushmore, but Lincoln opposed the idea. They
also discussed the Hall of Records.

It is right and fitting that a memorial plaque to Gutzon
Borglum be placed at Mount Rushmore. He devoted a large
part of the last sixteen years of his life to carving the four
faces on that mountain. Over a million visitors a year are
now coming to gaze at his work. In 1925, a thousand hardy
souls fought their way through the rugged hills and forests
of South Dakota to watch a dreamer plant an American
flag atop Mount Rushmore and to listen in disbelief while
he talked of carving a page from America's history on that
rugged rock. As early as 1914, long before he dreamed of the
four faces on Mount Rushmore, Gutzon wrote, "We have
not begun as a people to realize that things we desired honestly
—liberty of conscience, freedom from European governments
and from the stain of slavery—were things to be proud of
things to sing about; to talk about; to write about; to build
around and build into our civic memorials; that they are
ours and that they belong to no one else, and that these
things and these things alone make us immortal. If we have
any art of any kind in song, in letters, in color, in stone or

bronze, it should tell about these things; it should write them in bold lines annually across the page of our own history."

Twelve thousand came in 1940 to see Gutzon unveil Theodore Roosevelt, the fourth face to emerge from the mountain. And now, in a single day, oftentimes more than ten thousand visit Mount Rushmore to gaze on Gutzon Borglum's story of the growth and expansion of our great country.

"Yes," Gutzon wrote in his memoirs in 1940, "my dream had come true. There, on the mountain top, as near to Heaven as we could make it, we have carved portraits of our leaders, that posterity and civilization may see hundreds of thousands of years hence what manner of men our leaders were, with a prayer and a belief that there among the clouds they may stand forever, where wind and rain alone shall wear them away."

Acknowledgments

One of the greatest joys in the preparation of this book was my association with the family and friends of Gutzon Borglum. I am deeply indebted to Lincoln and Louella Borglum for so graciously inviting me into their home and allowing me unlimited use of the vast collection of letters, writings, diaries, scrapbooks, and pictures of Gutzon and Mary Borglum. I am also indebted to Mrs. Mary Ellis Vhay for sharing with me reminiscences of her mother and father.

Friends, acquaintances, and co-workers of Gutzon Borglum gave generously of their time to discuss with me their experiences with Mr. Borglum. Others allowed me the use of personal correspondence. I am especially grateful for the help given me by Russell M. Arundel, Luigi Del Bianco, United States Senator Francis Case, Charles d'Emery, Miss Angna Enters, Mrs. Marion Bell Fairchild, Supreme Court Justice Felix Frankfurter, Gerald W. Johnson, Mrs. A. C. Jones, Frank C. Marsh, Josef Meier, and Mrs. Jean Philip Mitchell.

Staff workers in libraries, art galleries, historical societies, and other associations greatly facilitated my research. To the Manuscript Division of the Library of Congress I owe a debt of gratitude for the many courtesies extended me during the months I spent in the Library going through the Borglum papers. I wish also to thank the Fine Arts Department and the Children's Section of the Open Shelf Department of the Boston Public Library and the Columbus Memorial Library of the Pan American Union for their help. I gratefully acknowledge valuable assistance given by The Corcoran Gallery of Art, Washington, D.C., The Joslyn Art Museum, Omaha, Nebraska, and The Metropolitan Museum of Art. Help was also given me by the Illinois Historical Society and the South

Dakota State School of Mines. The Idaho State Historical Society, the Genealogical Society, Church of Jesus Christ of Latter Day Saints, and The Reverend Father Anthony J. Fresnak, St. Patrick's Church, Fremont, Nebraska, aided me in my search for information on early Borglum family records.

Members of the National Park Service were most helpful in supplying information concerning the carving of the four faces on Mount Rushmore. My heartfelt thanks to Conrad Wirth, Director, for his friendly encouragement and to Roy E. Appleman, Staff Historian, for his many helpful suggestions. I will long remember my visit to Mount Rushmore, where, at the kind invitation of Senator Francis Case, I attended a meeting of the Mount Rushmore National Memorial Commission. My special thanks to W. Leon Evans, Park Superintendent, Russell Apple, Park Historian, and to Park Rangers Robert Hunt and Van Hunnick for making my visit a memorable one.

I wish to thank the Honorable and Mrs. Hugh M. Milton and Mrs. H. B. Powell for their assistance in assembling material concerning Stone Mountain. Acknowledgment is also made to Miss Helen Keller and her publishers, Doubleday and Company, Inc., for permission to quote from *Helen Keller's Journal* her greeting to Mr. Borglum as given on page 196.

I will be eternally grateful to my very dear friends, Mrs. Douglas H. Dies and Mrs. Mollie Somerville, who gave so generously of their time and talents to do research for me at the Library of Congress after I left Washington, D.C. And to Mrs. Lillian McClintock, Editor, Children's Books, Rand McNally and Company, I owe a very real debt of gratitude for her fine editorial assistance.

And last, but by no means least, my heartfelt thanks to my son Jon, who shared so much in the making of this book, particularly in the assembling of the illustrations and the taking of the photograph of Mount Rushmore which was incorporated in the design of the jacket.

WILLADENE PRICE

Index

221